Hana na Maui, a copper plate engraving from the
Lahainaluna Seminary press, ca. 1836.

Hana was in those days a noted place famous for the fortified hill Ka'uiki, the surf at Puhele, the fresh water bathing pool of Kumaka, the diving at Waiohinu, the flying spray of Kama, the changing color of the fronds of ama'u fern, the yellow-leafed 'awa of Lanakila, the delicious poi of Kuakahi, the fat shellfish ('opihi) of Kawaipapa, the fat soft uhu fish of Haneo'o, and the juicy pork and tender dog meat dear to the memory of chiefs of that land, moistened by the 'apuakea rain that rattles on the hala trees from Wakiu to Honokalani.

—Samuel Manaiakalani Kamakau
in *Ruling Chiefs of Hawaii,* writing about
life in 18th Century Hana

ON THE HANA COAST

No nā kupa i makālae o Hāna ola ka noho ʻana a mau loa aku

Inquiries should be directed to:
Emphasis International Ltd./Link Inc.
10th Floor, Wilson House
19-27 Wyndham Street, Central
Hong Kong.

Typography by Innovative Media, Inc., Honolulu.
Printed in Hong Kong by Cameron Printing Company Limited.

ISBN: 962-7073-02-4

ON THE HANA COAST

Being an accounting of adventures,
past and present, in a land
where the hand of man
seems to rest
lightly

Produced and Directed by Leonard Lueras
Text by Ron Youngblood
With Editorial Contributions by
Beverly Creamer, Carl Lindquist and Ka'upena Wong
Project Editor: Peggy Bendet
Book Design: Fred Bechlen

Published by Emphasis International Ltd. and Carl Lindquist
Second Edition 1987

EDITORS' NOTES

On the Hana Coast every hill, plain and geographic dimple seems to spawn its own multiplicity of stories, its own legendary past. There is a massive volume of material available, some of it having the clear ring of authenticity and some of it highly suspect. Consequently, this book, like many "literary" endeavors, was written by a process of selection, and a lot had to be left out.

The book's main author, Ron Youngblood, drew from a rich variety of sources: a range of literature, personal interviews and visits to Hana—made by car, by motorcycle and on foot—over a period of ten years time. Youngblood's research was also complemented by his myriad experiences as a County of Maui information officer, newspaper editor, freelance writer and news broadcaster.

In the beginning Youngblood felt he was ultimately prepared to take on this literary adventure, but by the time the book was in its final editorial stages he admitted that he hadn't been. Writing *On the Hana Coast* became a metaphor for the entire Hāna Coast experience—or, in Youngblood's words, "a sensory overload, followed by a slow awakening and a growing consciousness. The Hāna Coast has shown through the centuries that it can be conquered, but, in the end, it is always the conqueror," he said.

Indeed, it was in—and with—such spirits that *On the Hana Coast* came to be written.

Other significant editorial contributions were made by Carl Lindquist, a son of Hawai'i, part-time resident of Hana, and the book's co-publisher; by Beverly Creamer, a reporter for *The Honolulu Advertiser* who recently spent a year researching the death of Charles Lindbergh in Hāna and its effect on the community; and by Ka'upena Wong, a "living treasure" of Hawai'i well-known for his knowledge of Hawaiian language and chants. Overall project editor was Peggy Bendet, a former reporter and editor for *The Honolulu Star-Bulletin* and for many years a writer and teacher with SYDA, an international educational foundation.

On the Hana Coast was produced and directed by Leonard Lueras, a roving, Honolulu-based journalist who in recent years has written, edited and published more than a dozen Pacific-related books. Lueras is editorial director of Emphasis International Ltd, the book's co-publisher.

The book's final design grid was created by Fred Bechlen, a Honolulu resident who does design work for *Fortune Magazine,* the Minolta camera company and other such prestige clients throughout the Pacific region. Other designers who worked on this project during its early and later stages were Steve Shrader and Terry Palumbo. The maps in the book's last section were prepared by Honolulu cartographer Rebecca Brown.

Artworks and photographs published in *On the Hana Coast* were gathered from a variety of sources, both current and archaic. Among contemporary contributors were Lueras, Dana Edmunds, Anselm Spring, Allan Seiden, Frank Salmoiraghi, Mary Ann Lynch, Steve Wilkings, Boone Morrison, Ronn Ronck, Ray Mains, Wendy Brody and Guy Buffet. Individual page-by-page credits for these contributors' works can be found in the book's last section.

Archive privileges, meanwhile, were generously offered by the Bernice Pauahi Bishop Museum, the Hawai'i State Archives, the Hawaiian Mission Children's Society Library, the new Hana Cultural Center, libraries of *The Honolulu Advertiser* and *The Honolulu Star-Bulletin,* the Soon family of Kau-pō, Maui, Honolulu antiquarian Don Severson, and Jean Mackenzie.

The Wanderer's creative staff would also like to acknowledge the support of Tom Chapman of Emphasis, Inc., Tokyo, and Steve Ellis of Emphasis (Hong Kong) Ltd, without whom this publishing venture would never have happened. Also important to the book's success were Betsy Altman and Elvis Loo of Emphasis, Hong Kong, who hand-carried the book through its final development and production stages.

Other persons we'd like to personally acknowledge include Babes Hanchett and Coila Eads of the Hana Cultural Center, Betty Kam and Debbie Dunn of the Bishop Museum's photo archives and Nedra Chung, who indexed the book. A special thank you also to our obliging cover model, Hana's inimitable Tiny Malaikini.

Ultimately, however, *On the Hana Coast* was created by Hana and her people. To these we would like to extend a warm *mahalo* plenty. And to all who crossed our publishing paths, *me ke aloha pumehana . . .*

CONTENTS

A lava flow meets the sea on the Kau-pō side of the Hāna Coast.

A Hāna-area waterfall cools a small valley, left, and below, rare silverswords march across the crater floor of Hale-a-ka-lā.

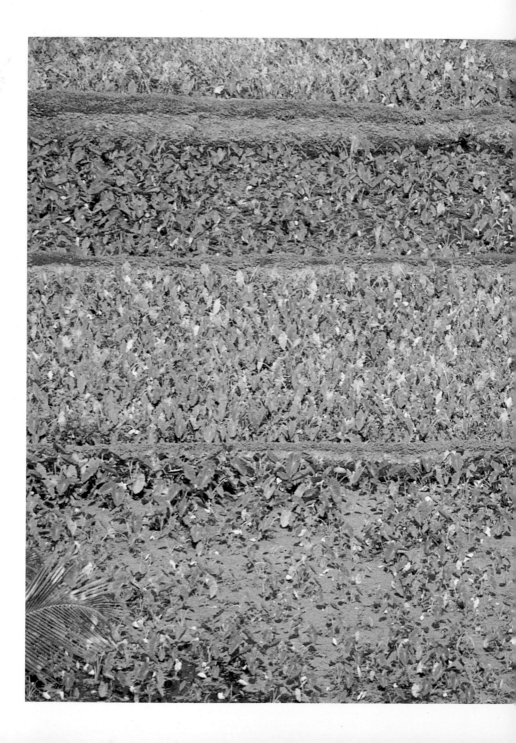

At Ke-ʻanae, taro farmers continue a centuries-old tradition by
cultivating living symbols of a reawakening culture.

Hāna's Malaikini family: (clockwise from bottom center)
Tiny, Lynette, Joe Sol, Paniani and Maedoria.

CHAPTER I

IN HAWAII'S 'HEARTLAND'
LOCAL FOLKS HAVE A 'WAY' ABOUT THEM

On the Hāna Coast there is the sea, the land and
"Out There", the rest of the world. Embraced by the sea
and protected by Hale-a-ka-lā, the "House of the Sun",
the Hāna Coast is an island on an island.

eographically, the Hāna Coast stretches from Ke-'anae on the north to Kau-pō on the south. Socially, the Hāna Coast life style extends from Pā'ia on the north to Hāna on the east and on around Hale-a-ka-lā to 'Ulu-pala-kua on the south. The sense of apartness is profound.

The sea and her sister, the rains, push and pound on the land, stripping away and building, just as the world pushes at the people who live in this "Heart of Hawaii". That pleasant nickname is on the bumper sticker of a dusty four-wheel drive vehicle which travels, happily, at 10 miles below the posted speed limit on an open, empty highway. Like the car, Hāna time moves slow, but "by and by" everything gets done and everyone gets somewhere.

Local Hawaiians have always known more about "Out There" than outsiders, the *haole*, have known about the Hāna Coast. But unlike many islanders, people of the Hāna Coast simply smile at the wonders of the outside world, content to live in their own special way in their own special place.

The people of the Hāna Coast do have a way about them. In almost any crowd anyplace else the folks from the Hāna Coast are easy to spot. There is a sense of relaxed apartness as they walk, slowly, seeming to savor whatever experience is at hand.

They gather in groups formed by family

and age delineations. The very young among them seem to fear nothing, having been treated with love and respect from earliest awareness. The older young adopt a kind of slouching swagger, as if realizing their distinction. The adults make a kind of celebration out of having gone *holoholo*, on an outing. You get the impression a party is always close at hand.

Generally speaking, you can strike no more generalities about the individuals who are of the Hāna Coast than you can, generally, about any collection of souls. There are only tendencies.

The people of the Hāna Coast tend to listen more than they talk, and they listen with more than their ears.

A Kona storm is blowing up and over the Kau-pō Peninsula. Rain water washes into gullies and then roars out to sea, slashing across the roadway. At a low spot in the road, a homeward-bound rancher is halted by a 30- to 40-foot wide jumble of rocks and brown, snarling water.

A man stands on the other side of the torrent, which is 18 inches deep and flowing fast enough to knock him down. He offers to help with the crossing by sighting along the bottom of the rancher's Land Cruiser and guiding its vulnerable underparts around the jumble of rocks and through the raging water.

Taking hand signals from the friend —

although he might have been an acquaintance, it's all the same on the Hāna Coast— the rancher is able to thread the Land Cruiser through the shoals to the other side.

The rancher thanks the helpful bystander, who merely shrugs in reply. Then the two of them pause in the rain to discuss the weather and the flooded sections of road. They stand a comfortable three feet apart, apparently studying their feet. To minds attuned to narrow-band verbalization, the silence during the conversation is deafening. In 15 minutes not more than a dozen words are spoken. To an essential word, the men add a shift of the body, a tilt of the head, a look, and one hundred other subtle, non-spoken signals.

On the Hāna Coast there is communication of a type most often seen in other places, other cultures, between long married couples. It is a sensing, a knowing, that allows one person to finish the other person's sentence.

Smile honestly, from the inside out, at a person from the Hāna Coast, and the natural reaction will be an honest smile in return.

That is, if you get close enough.

Most visitors get their first and sometimes last glimpse of Hāna through the windows of a no-mileage, flat-rate rental car.

A tourist couple from "Out There" decides to take the ride in to Hāna from Central Maui. A short distance out of Pā'ia, a straight road with broad shoulders begins to undulate, but the real curves are still miles ahead.

The man and woman love the scenery— but only when they snatch their eyes away from the 15 yards of pavement directly in front of the car's hood.

"The scenery is lovely," she says. "Be careful of that jeep with the fishing poles ahead."

"Yes, dear," he says. "This road is terrible. I hope it improves," he adds as they

The *hukilau* is a community event in Kī-pahulu.

take the sweeping turns down into Māliko Gulch.

Later, at Huelo, the road dives into gully-rimming twists and turns of the "real" road to Hāna.

"This is a road?" he asks.

"Watch your rear view mirror," she warns, reading from a pamphlet. "When a car or cars are following, pull off the road."

"Pull over where?" he wonders, noticing a car five feet off his rear bumper. "There's nothing but cliff on one side and ocean on the other."

They arrive at a one-lane bridge which has a little turn-out space. He pulls off to the side. The car behind follows him off the road. They're tourists, too.

A little farther down the road, she reads from the pamphlet again: "It says here you should keep to your side of the road."

"But there isn't any road on our side," he counters.

"Is the gas tank full?"

"We should have enough if I can ever get out of first gear," he says.

The little car swings around a curve and goes across another of the 56 one-lane bridges on the road to Hāna.

"The pamphlet says we should stop often to rest," she says.

"We'll stop at the next park," he replies, not knowing there is no next park.

"Please, can we stop someplace," she pleads. "I'm getting dizzy from watching the trees as we go around corners."

"In a minute. As soon as we get to some straight road," he replies, not knowing there is no straight road.

And once there, he had to drive back.

The Hāna Coast is an intensely personal experience, a sensory overload that gives way with the passage of time to a kind of understanding that enriches. It has been said that love is impossible without understanding and that understanding is impossible without knowledge. On the Hāna

Horseback riders descend through morning mists
in Hale-a-ka-lā Crater.

Coast, knowledge is as elusive as the mists that shroud the upper valleys where soft tradewinds impact with black lava *pali,* spectacular palisades formed when the island went through its birth pangs.

But as the sun burns away the mists, revealing the verdure of the mountainsides, knowledge comes to those who approach the Hāna Coast with a readiness to cast aside ideas molded by different lands, different cultures. Beneath the riot of plants, underneath the sweeping fields of pasture grass, the land bears the scars of natural violence that still visits on the wings of winter storms and with the smash of surf against rock on the shore. Behind the calm eyes of the people of the Hāna Coast, behind the easy smiles, are hundreds of years of political and social turmoil usually hidden from all but those who look closely. It is a land that has been fought over, abused, protected and cherished.

There is an intangible "something"

about the Hāna Coast that has been at work since the first Marquesans sailed here from the South Pacific. Through hundreds of years of Hawaiian history, Hāna's *mana,* her power, has worked its spell on arrogant chiefs, wise poets and clever tellers of tales. The tides of Hawaiian political affairs repeatedly swept across Hāna, as rulers from the Big Island and Central Maui coveted her rich stands of timber and fertile valleys—resources that meant wealth and power.

Then, on the same trackless ocean routes discovered by northerly bound Polynesian seafarers, came Europeans questing for new lands, new wealth, new power. They, in turn, were followed by emissaries from the Christian world. These stern-visaged Calvinists and visionary Catholics came and saw a land that tested their souls with temptation and tribulation. But even as they bent the land and the people to their will, the conquerors were themselves conquered.

Ranching is a major business on the Hāna Coast. This particular
paniolo hails from Haleakala Ranch.

The *mana* of the Hāna Coast continued to work through decades of relative isolation. Native populations shrank, year by year, and yet some hardy souls found a way to hang on. The industrial age arrived on the Hāna Coast, and with it came contract laborers imported by the shipload from China, Japan, Portugal, the Philippines. The new arrivals borrowed methods that had worked for the Hawaiians before them, and they, too, became a part of the Hāna Coast—more layers in a society that is not so much a melting pot as a parfait.

Today, as in the past, the adventurer and the escapist travel to the Hāna Coast for a firsthand look at a fabled place. Today, as in the past, the Hāna Coast is home—a place to bear children and hold hopes for the future. In that dichotomy of traveler and resident there is a symbiotic tie: each supplies what the other needs. The traveler brings the basic resource the community cannot itself supply—money. The resident offers and seeks to preserve what the traveler can find in few other places—a largely natural and benevolent environment.

Much of the charm of Hāna comes from its diversity: One side of the mountain is drenched to drowning while the other greedily laps up morning dew for lack of other moisture. The "Wild West" lives here, in the form of *paniolo,* working cowboys, who sometimes herd their cattle past the country manses of resident celebrities, transplanted "natives" from London, Hollywood and Manhattan who delight in Hāna's hang-the-cost solitude and comfort.

The latest in television sets, linked to Earth-girdling satellites, sit under the rusted corrugated roofs of houses handbuilt by the people who live in them.

In one place on the Hāna Coast, a man and his family live as his father and his father and his father before him; in another place, a man makes wine from pineapples. And yet somewhere else, ruby lasers scan

Hale-a-ka-lā's chilly skies only a few miles from where early Hawaiians chipped weapons and tools in secret flint quarries.

The Hāna Coast experience is as far away as another language and as close as a lover's whisper.

No matter where you are on the Hāna Coast, just over your shoulder is the 7,000-foot giant, Hale-a-ka-lā, a geologically youngish mountain crowned by a crater that has astounded and awed man ever since the first Polynesian used it as a shortcut from one side of the island to the other.

In the crater, time slows to the labored beat and pulse of sea-level heart and lungs working in the elevated thinness of its atmosphere.

In the northwest corner, there is a cabin and space for tent camping. The spot is a couple of hours' walk from the bottom of Hale-mau'u Trail, one of three routes into the cathedral-like grandeur that is the crater. The silence is palpable. Occasionally there

Legend says that days are born in Hale-a-ka-lā.

are whispers of wind or the mild complaint of flies, but nothing else.

The campground at Hale-mau'u is on a grassy slope that makes for easy sleeping. The cabin, with water and sanitary facilities, is farther down the slope and slightly tucked back into a crease in the rim wall.

The night sky is a comfortable inky black, spangled with stars undimmed by man-made effluents. Thirty-degree temperatures before dawn make the first cup of coffee and a heavy sweater delightful. The idea is to watch the day aborning from inside the crater. The seconds build into minutes as the sky slides through a new-day-coming spectrum—grey to rose to orange to yellow. From this spot at this time of year (August), the arriving sun is framed precisely by the square-sided rim cut by Kau-pō Gap, a sight so loaded with serendipity it seems preordained.

It's as if the walls of the gap are cradling the infant day, making it welcome on the Hāna Coast.

As the day grows in maturity, the sun throws its rays across the arid proliferation that is the floor of the crater to the far wall, which, like the sun's entryway, is a gap: the Ko'olau Gap, the top of Ke-'anae Valley.

The two gaps link the crater directly to the Hāna Coast, making them two of the most important geological features of the area for early Hawaiians. These gaps allowed Maui's earliest settlers to establish land routes across the island when seasonal storms made travel along the coast by canoe hazardous, if not impossible.

The island of Maui has been described by many as the torso and head of a human figure—some say male, some say female. In either case, the Hāna Coast girds the loins of this lusty Pacific child island.

An ancient *mele,* handwritten in a notebook and found in an abandoned house, pictures Hāna as "'ā ina ua lani ha 'aha 'a," "the land of rain and the low-lying sky." She is that—and much more.

A Man Named Solomon

Not far past the turnoff to the Hāna Airport, a rocky road plunges off to the right and disappears into the thick undergrowth. Here the *hala, kukui,* mango, guava, papaya, banana, ferns and gingers of every description are woven into a verdant tapestry.

This is a place revered since ancient times, its *mele* telling of an abundance of streams, ponds and waterfalls. A pool called Puna-lu'u is located here, and it is said that in the old days passing *ali'i* would stop to bathe in its cool, refreshing waters.

This is the birthplace and the home of my old friend Solomon Hoopai.

The widowed patriarch of a large family, Sol returned here after his career as a rigger on a drilling crew had carried him to many other corners of the world. Here he gathers his children, his memories and the ways of his elders around him like a fine *kapa.* Today, he has invited me to go with him to net *āhole,* a delectable silver fish which lives in the brackish water found where streams empty into the ocean.

It is 5 a.m. and, typical of Hāna mornings, there is a light rain—*noenoe uakea o Hāna,* the white rain of Hāna.

Sol is waiting in the road at the front of his small wooden house, a blue nylon net slung over his shoulder. Shirtless and barefoot, his dark, strong body belies the fact that he will be 75 this year.

We park at the top of a small rise, running parallel to the stream, and I follow him in a crouching walk down the trail to the black rock shoreline. The tide is high, and there is a crashing surf. The fresh and salt water co-mingle, surging in foam around our legs.

Sol loosens the rope binding the net, hands me one end and moves quickly across the stream to anchor the other with a large rock. Staying low, he comes back sure-footed across the slippery stone bottom, motioning me to kneel and telling me to hold the net tight and low in the churning water.

He walks to the top of the rise, near the jeep, hesitates only a moment, and then leaps almost to the middle of the cold black pool, flailing his arms, shouting and slapping the water as he moves downstream. It is the old Hawaiian stratagem, *pa'ipa'i,* to frighten the fish into making a run for the sea.

I feel one fish hit the net, then another and another, and by the time Sol reaches me there are five in all, each longer than a man's forearm.

"Good," he says, "not too much, and all big kind." Sol believes, as do many Hawaiians, that taking more fish than can be readily used will result in poor catches for many days to come.

On the opposite bank, there is watercress growing where a spring bubbles out over a small ledge. Sol says that he planted the patch there more than 50 years ago and hands me a knife, telling me to cut some to go in the bag with the fish.

Then he walks down to the breaking surf, soon returning with another bulging bag—full of *'opihi* and *limu,* shellfish and seaweed.

We return to his house and clean our fish, Sol insisting that I take the two largest, loading my back seat with a large stalk of bananas and handing me a newspaper-wrapped package of *kūlolo,* a taro and coconut cream pudding. He reminds me that both *'ulu* (breadfruit) and mango are plentiful right now, and lashes a long bamboo pole to the roof of my jeep, to be used for picking on the way back to the highway.

A quick, cold beer is next—Sol laughs and says this is his Listerine—then the embrace and *aloha* of old friends, and I drive away into the soft morning sunlight . . . my thoughts on this good Hawaiian man and the generous bounty of the land that is his home.

—Carl Lindquist

Solomon Hoopai.

Pō'ele, pō'ele'ele i ka pō,
E ho'onū la i ke anu,
'Ōlapa ka uila, he kaula,
Ku'i hekili, kani a 'u'ina,
'Oni ka honua, naue ka moku.
Ua la'i.
Ki'eki'e mai 'Eleao,
Moku ka pawa, he alaula.
Kukuna lā pā i ka la'i,
I ka piko o ka mauna.
Nani wale 'o Haleakalā,
No Maui o Papa i ke kapu.

Darkness, intense darkness at night,
The wind moans in the cold,
Lightning flashes, a streak of light,
Thunder peals, lightning and thunder,
The earth moves, the island shakes.
Silence.
Regally stands 'Eleao,
Day breaks, dawn glows.
Sun rays reach out in the calm,
On the mountain's summit.
How beautiful is Haleakalā,
Belonging to Maui in the sacred lap of Papa.

—KA'UPENA WONG

Cinder cones in Hale-a-ka-lā are sculptured remnants of fiery
volcanic activity. The last such eruption took place about 1790.

CHAPTER II

THE EVOLUTION OF AN ISLAND
FARTHER FROM ANYPLACE THAN ANYPLACE ELSE

For more than 200 million years after the Earth's
major land masses were well established, only water
rolled and churned where the Hawaiian Islands now
stand in splendid isolation.

Polynesian chronicles, handed down from storyteller to storyteller throughout the Pacific Basin, and modern-day geologists explain the islands' creation in ways more similar than not. Island bards sing of a time when the Earth was hot and liquid and surrounded by darkness. Scientists speak of a time beginning 25 million years ago when the Hawaiian Island chain was thrust up rudely out of the womb of the Earth, as the planet's crust moved in a smooth and continuous process of birth that spanned 20 million years.

Polynesian chants tell of a long night slipping away and, with its passage, the coming of a time of turmoil and a time of calm, when the Earth rose and held up the sky.

Geologists say there is a spot on the Earth's crust, directly below the Big Island of Hawai'i, where magma searches for cracks in the Pacific Plate moving slowly overhead, two or three inches a year. In this way the Hawaiian Islands were born, one by one. The Big Island, with its currently active Kī-lau-ea Volcano, is the youngest of the litter; Kure Atoll, 1,500 miles to the northwest, is the oldest.

The sea fought the arrival of the new land with the heat-dissipating pressure of more than five miles of water, which made the young rock dense and hardy. As quickly as the sea cooled the magma, the pressure from the Earth's core squeezed more magma out. So it was that mountains were raised from a sea which immediately began reclaiming them, directly and indirectly—directly by smashing their shores with waves, tides and currents; indirectly through rains that eroded and washed the land back into the sea.

Although several million years old, Maui is a young island, the consequence of the mating of two adjoining islands. West Maui is the older. The Hāna Coast fringes the younger, with Hale-a-ka-lā at its core.

Hale-a-ka-lā Mountain came to be in three stages.

First there was an upthrusting from the sea floor that shoved land into the air. A spate of lava, known as the Honomanū Volcanic Series, joined the upstart to the older West Maui volcanic range at the isthmus, the spacious plain between them.

Then came another series of copious lava flows from gigantic cinder cones which had formed along the rifts—this known as the Kula Volcanic Series—mantling the earlier flows to a thickness of 2,500 feet at the summit. Following this was a quiet time, when rains went about their work, creating rivulets that grew into gullies and then into valleys, some of them 5,000 feet deep.

The most recent stage is a series of eruptions known as the Hāna Volcanic Series, which began with a rift opening across the

Lau'ae fern.

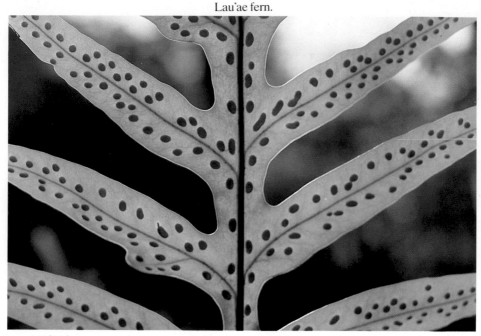

mountain between what are now Hāna Town and La Pérouse Bay. The Hāna flows, welling out along the rift, covered the earlier Kula lavas. These later flows were immense, filling the region between the heads of Kau-pō and Ke-'anae valleys to a depth of about 3,000 feet, plugging up the headlands of the valleys, washing up against the sides and flowing toward the sea, creating the peninsulas that mark Kau-pō and Ke-'anae today.

Hale-a-ka-lā may have yet another stage of volcanic activity; geologists label it a dormant volcano, not an extinct one. Recent work by the U.S. Geological Survey indicates the latest volcanic action at Hāna came within the last 500 years, well after the Polynesians arrived. It has been chronicled by them in various tales about wrathful gods.

The last eruption on Maui is dated at about 1790, 22 years after the visit of the English naval captain James Cook. Evidence of this eruption is documented in maps drawn by two explorers, the French Rear Adm. Jean-Francois Galaup, Comte de La Pérouse, who landed on the south shore of Hale-a-ka-lā in 1786, and the British Capt. George Vancouver, who visited the same area in 1792. La Pérouse's carefully drawn maps showed a shallow bay, but six years later Vancouver noted that fresh lava flows had surrounded the bay, now named after La Pérouse. That eruption fed a three-mile wide flow, which swept down from two vents through what was probably a populated area since the Hawaiians established villages there almost immediately afterwards.

Today the post-natal pangs of Hale-a-ka-lā's birth form one of the most desolate and beautiful sections of the Hāna Coast, a welcome landing for chance visitors.

Everything on the Hāna Coast, as elsewhere in Hawai'i, is an immigrant. Considering that Hawai'i Nei lies roughly 2,000 miles from any appreciable land mass—

Naupaka finds root in a seaside lava flow.

farther away from anyplace than anyplace else on the globe — it is a marvel that these islands are anything more than bare, crumbling rock. And yet . . .

The native plants of the islands are a remarkable collection of oddities, some of them evolutes found only in Hawai'i—for example, giant ferns and herbs with leaves up to six feet in diameter. Such island endemics, life forms shaped by time, chance and isolation, are traced to some 275 species that drifted in at a rate of about one every 70,000 years since the land first emerged from the sea. These were the natural immigrants that arrived unaided by man—carried by the wind, the sea and by hardy birds. These plants are found now only in remote regions: the walls of isolated valleys, the rugged cliffs and mountain ridges of a terrain like that of the Hāna Coast.

One spectacular native plant, the silversword or *Argyroxiphium sandwicense,*

grows only on the slopes of Hale-a-ka-lā and at Mauna Kea on the Big Island. This distant and quite exotic relative of the sunflower has long silvery leaves forming a rosette, sometimes two feet in diameter, at its base, a six-foot stalk and a cluster of close to a hundred purplish daisy-like flowers. In bloom, the silversword has the appearance of a mammoth visitor from another world, thriving as it does in the heady air of the mountains and on a bed of stark lava rock.

There are also plants that developed woody species in Hawai'i although members of the same family elsewhere in the world are delicate herbs.

Botanists believe most of the plant life in the islands has its origin in tropical Asia and Indonesia, with a few species from North and South America. What happened to the plants once they arrived is a story unique to Hawai'i.

The Hāna Coast has been shaped by the forces of fire and stone, capricious nature and the hand of man.

Interior palisades, or *pali,* Hale-a-ka-lā.

Man's conquest of the Hawaiian Islands began sometime between 500 and 800 A.D.

A band of seafaring island people, already boasting a history of long ocean voyages, set sail in the Marquesas and headed north.

Perhaps it was the migratory land birds they saw flying in from the north that piqued their interest in the possibility of new lands to conquer.

Perhaps it was the success of past explorations that gave them the confidence to strike out across open oceans in their double-hulled canoes.

Most likely, those long-ago Polynesian seafarers were guided by the ocean and the sky, natural charts studied by father and son through generations spent voyaging toward empty horizons.

One thing is sure: Long before the Vikings set sail, and with no instruments but their own senses, Polynesians from the Marquesas found and created the oldest

known settlements in the Hawaiian Islands, some 2,400 miles from their original South Pacific home.

While the most likely first landfall would have been the Big Island, certainly one of the first places to be touched of the other islands would have been Hāna.

With its deep valleys, shore plains and abundant water, and with the blessing of reliable tradewinds out of the northeast, there are more than a few similarities between the wet areas of the Hāna Coast and the home islands of those first Polynesian settlers.

To establish themselves on the new islands, they brought with them in their canoes a range of crop plants (domesticated species primarily of Southeast Asian origin, such as taro, yams, bananas and breadfruit) and breeding populations of domestic animals (the pig, dog and jungle fowl, a kind of chicken).

During a period of nearly 600 years of apparently undisturbed and isolated development, the Marquesans and their descen-

Cinder cone, near Mākena.

dants established viable economics on islands which, until they arrived, held little or nothing that could be eaten, except for the abundant supplies of fish, turtles and nesting seabirds provided by the sea.

The Hawaiians have been noted in recent times for living in harmony with nature, an attitude developed in their earliest years in these islands. During the period from 1100 to 1300 A.D., they evolved a system of rotating crops that took into account the carrying capacity of a finite amount of land and, also, a method of marine harvest that allowed the resources of the sea to renew themselves. An example of the latter is the Hawaiian method of picking *'opihi,* a conical shaped mollusk that lives on wave-dashed rocks. To this day it is *kapu* for Hawaiians to pick all of the *'opihi* off any given boulder—a prohibition which assures a future supply.

The chants of this time describe a constant coming and going between Hawai'i and islands to the south, principally the So-ciety Islands (Tahiti). On the south side of the Hāna Coast there is a channel between Maui, Ka-ho'olawe and Lā-na'i which the Hawaiians called Ke-ala-i-Kahiki. The name can be transliterated into *te-ala-itahiti,* "The Pathway to Tahiti" or "The Pathway to Foreign Lands."

The Society Islanders and the Marquesans were both branches of the Polynesian family, and they shared a common language, enjoyed similar foods and related to similar myths, deities and cultural peculiarities. Yet it is thought by some scholars that the new wave of Polynesians subjugated the earlier settlers and/or drove them north in the Hawaiian chain until they were assimilated or destroyed.

After 1300 A.D., about the time of King Arthur's Camelot, these trans-oceanic voyages seem to have stopped, and the Hawaiian Islands again settled into an active isolation. It was during this time that Hawaiian society evolved to its economic and cultural zenith.

A society as complex as that the Hawaiians established before the coming of western man required a continuity that spanned generations.

The islanders developed no verifiable writing form, but they did preserve rich, detailed verbal accounts in their *mele* which traced mythology, genealogy, religion and political events.

The Hawaiians placed events in time in these chants with references to genealogies and the eras of specific rulers. Calendar dates have since been overlayed, primarily through the efforts of Abraham Fornander, a 19th Century scholar and Maui Circuit Court judge considered one of the most reliable scribes of pre-written history in Hawaii.

Fornander sent legmen tramping the hills and shorelines of Hawai'i, recording chants handed down by the *kūpuna,* the elders. Using his own fluency in the language, Fornander translated the chants and, estimating 30 years per generation,

"dated" many of the events they described. His method of dating was later substantiated by archeological research.

Drawing on Fornander's *An Account of the Polynesian Race,* a three-volume work published in London between 1879 and 1885, and Martha Beckwith's translation, *The Kumulipo, A Hawaiian Creation Chant,* first published by the University of Chicago Press in 1951, it is possible to sketch a socio-political history of Hawai'i and, specifically, the Hāna Coast.

The *Kumulipo* blends three tales of the origin of mankind. The three explanations overlap, appearing to be variants of a common source. It has been suggested that they represent the way in which different branches of a family line evolve from their ancestral origins.

The Hawaiians put a great deal of importance on genealogy, and their chant of creation indicates why. The *Kumulipo,* which some say was commissioned by the Hawaiian King Ka-lā-kaua to establish his

White foam and black lava, on the Hāna Coast.

own indisputable right of sovereignty, traces the ancestry of the Hawaiian *ali'i,* the ruling class, and the king's own family line directly back to the creative source.

The *Kumulipo* is not the Hawaiians' only account of creation, but it is the best known and is probably the most accurate reflection of ancient Hawaiian belief.

According to the *Kumulipo,* after the creation there is a period of darkness. The night gives birth to Kumulipo, man, and Pō'ele, woman; darkness persists while plants and animals are born. Day comes in the eighth chant of the *Kumulipo* and with its light comes the Hawaiian gods.

Other creation stories differ at their outset, but generally agree on the birth of Wā-kea, the sky father, and Papa, the earth mother, the human ancestors from whom all Hawaiian *ali'i* are descended.

Stemming from Wākea and Papa are two major Hawaiian genealogies: the Nana-'ulu and the 'Ulu. The Nana-'ulu is the wellspring for the *ali'i* of O'ahu and Kaua'i. The 'Ulu line supplied the chiefs of Maui and the Big Island.

One descendant of the 'Ulu line who has a particularly notorious place in the history of the Hāna Coast was Hua. This powerful 12th Century *mō'ī,* king, of East Maui is reputed to have brought about a three-year scourge of drought and famine that ravaged not only Maui but also half of the Big Island and, to lesser extents, the other islands.

In Hawai'i's surviving records there are some blank spots regarding the various rulers of Maui after the 12th Century.

In those times there were two separate kingdoms on Maui, and it wasn't until nearly three centuries later, under Pi'i-lani, that the Hāna Coast was united politically with the central and west-end portions of the island.

During the 300 years between Hua and Pi'i-lani in the mid 15th Century, it seems that a family of the Nana-'ulu line was in

Hua, Hāna's Infamous King

The legend of Hua, a 12th Century king of Hāna, is a powerful lesson in royal responsibility. Hua is described as reckless, independent, warlike and a lover of revelries. Since he had access to the largest and finest timber in the area, his war canoes were abundant and formidable. When not harrassing his frontiers, which stretched from Ke-'anae to Kaupō, he made raids on the Big Island and Moloka'i.

Hua's high priest was Lua-ho'omoe, who claimed to be an *ikū pau*, a direct descendant of Kāne, one of the principal gods in the Hawaiian pantheon. Lua-ho'omoe didn't think much of Hua's warlike ways and counseled him to pursue more peaceful ventures, a move which, in a realm of absolute rulers, nettled this particular king.

The sovereign of the Hāna Coast fell to blaming his occasional failures on the battlefield to Lua-ho'omoe. It is said that following an unsuccessful raid on Moloka'i Hua forbade the use of a spring that had been set aside for Lua-ho'omoe's *heiau* and speared a black *kapu* hog being raised for a sacrifice. When Lua-ho'omoe objected, the king threatened the high priest with the hog's fate.

Later, when Hua raised taxes in the kingdom and Lua-ho'omoe and his followers sided with the protesting population, the king looked for a way he could be rid of the meddlesome priest.

Hua decided to lay a trap, ordering his men to snare *'ua'u,* a water bird, but limiting their hunt to the mountains. The hunters, in the presence of both Hua and Lua-ho'omoe, asked if it were possible to find seabirds in the mountains.

An account of the exchange that followed was recorded in 1888 by King Ka-lā-kaua in his book *The Myths and Legends of Hawaii: The Fables and Folk-lore of a Strange People:*

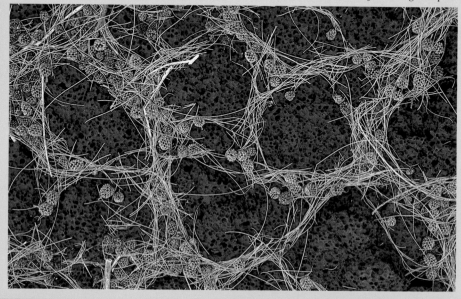

"Do you inquire of me?" asked the priest, after a pause, and finding the king did not answer.

"I inquire of any one who thinks he knows," returned the man in charge of the hunt.

"Then the birds you seek will not be found in the mountains at this season of the year," returned the priest, "and you must set your snares by the sea shore."

"Is it so that you would attempt to countermand my orders?" exclaimed Hua, in apparent anger. "I order my servants to go to the mountains for the 'ua'u, and you tell them to set their snares by the sea shore!"

"I humbly ask the king to remember that I have given no orders," calmly replied the priest.

"But you have dared to interfere with mine!" retorted the king. "Now listen. My men shall go to the mountains in search of the birds I require. If they find them there, I will have you slain as a false prophet and misleader of the people!"

The next day the bird hunters returned with their catch and declared that the seabirds had, indeed, been snared in the mountains, even though they had really gone to the only place they could be found, the shore.

Lua-ho'omoe sought to prove this point by slitting open the birds' crops and showing Hua the small fish and bits of seaweed he found in them.

Hua was enraged. He seized a javelin and, without a word, savagely drove it into the breast of Lua-ho'omoe, killing him on the spot.

What happened next stands as one of the most vivid examples of what the gods in the Hawaiian pantheon could do when the social structure was threatened by the breaking of one of Hawaii's greatest kapu—violence against a priest.

As translated by Ka-lā-kaua, the mele says:

The earth was affected with a slight but continuous tremor; a hot and almost suffocating wind had set in from the southward; strange murmurs were heard in the air; the skies were crimson and drops of blood fell from the clouds; and finally reports came from all parts of Hāna that the streams, wells and springs were no longer yielding water, and a general flight of the people to the mountains had commenced.

Hua tried to make amends but the new high priest, a son of the slain Lua-ho'omoe, refused to cooperate and disappeared. Another high priest was named. Sacrifices were made, including the baking of humans in an imu kālua loa. Construction was begun on a new heiau but there weren't enough people to complete the arduous labor.

The drought continued. Hua fled to Kona on the Big Island and the drought followed him. He moved from place to place for more than three years, afflicting almost half of the Big Island with the drought before dying of thirst and starvation.

Ka-lā-kaua quoted an old Hawaiian saying—"rattling are the bones of Hua in the sun," or "dry are the bones of Hua in the sun"—which refers to the fate of one high in power who defies the gods and persecutes the priesthood. That Hua's sacrilege also afflicted the other islands when his followers tried to escape the scourge by fleeing Hāna was seen as evidence throughout the land that everyone was punished by the transgressions of an ali'i.

control of the Hāna Coast. The rest of the island, meanwhile, was ruled by descendants of the Maui 'Ulu line, and it wasn't a good time for the *maka'āinana,* the common Hawaiian, due to the persistent efforts of each ruler to become *mō'ī* of all Maui.

It is known that Kāke'a established a court at Lahaina about 1360 A.D. and that he was succeeded by a son, Ka-hekili I, who was, in turn, succeeded by Kāwao-kāō-hele. It is thought that during the time of Kāwao-kāō-hele or his son and successor, Pi'i-lani, the Hāna Coast came under their control, thus unifying Maui under one family of *ali'i.*

Pi'i-lani's rule is remembered as a time of unity, peace, prosperity and construction of public works, including, at Ka-'elekū, the largest *heiau* in existence. A *heiau* is a Hawaiian place of worship, usually a platform of earthen terraces or laboriously assembled stones.

Although Pi'i-lani kept his court "Out There" in Lahaina and Wai-luku, he maintained a home in Hāna. Even then it was a place of physical and spiritual refuge.

Pi'i-lani ordered the construction of fish ponds and irrigation systems for the taro fields, and he undertook the immense task of building a network of stone-paved roads, four to six feet wide, around and across the island. The job was continued by his son, Kiha-a-pi'ilani, who extended the ribbon of coastal road first built in Hāna around to West Maui and also up Kau-pō Gap through the crater.

Kiha-a-pi'ilani was followed by his son Kama-lālā-walu, who is said to have sent his son to spy on the Big Island. The young man reported the island was undefended. Kama-lālā-walu invaded with an enormous army, found many people and was annihilated with his forces by the Hawai'i chief.

The Maui line passed to Kauhi-a-kama, and followed, from father to son, to Ka-lani-kau-māka'o-wākea to Lono-honua-

kini to Kāula-hea to Ke-kaulike to Ka-me-hameha-nui to Ka-hekili, the last of the Maui kings.

Around 1759, the Hāna Coast once again rang with battle cries and the fierce grunting of warriors locked in mortal combat. As a result of this great struggle, the Big Island's ruler, Ka-lani-'ōpu'u, captured and held Hāna for more than 20 years. His stronghold was Ka-'uiki, the fortress hill guarding the south side of Hāna Bay.

In about 1780, Ka-hekili sent two forces of warriors against Ka-lani-'ōpu'u. According to Fornander, Ka-hekili's army attacked by way of Kau-pō and the Ko'olau mountains in Ke-'anae. He could have done this by sending fleets of canoes to Kau-pō and Ke-'anae and then fighting on land from there. He also could have sent armies overland by having them hike up Hale-a-ka-lā, into the crater and out Kau-pō and the Ko'olau gaps on the paved foot highways that existed. Or, he could have done—and probably did—both.

The early skirmishes resolved down to a siege of Ka-'uiki. According to Fornander's account in *The Polynesian Race:*

> The Hawaii chiefs were well provisioned and the fort held out stoutly until Kahekili was advised to cut off the water supply of the fort by damming and diverting the springs in the neighborhood. The measure succeeded, and the garrison, making desperate sorties beyond their lines to procure water, were slain in numbers and finally surrendered, expecting no mercy and obtaining none . . . large numbers of Hawaii chiefs and soldiers were slain and their corpses burnt at Kuawalu and at Honuaula *(heiau).*

While monumental events swirled through the islands, life for the residents of

Torch ginger, Hāna town.

Queen Ka-ʻahu-manu in an 1816 sketch by Louis Choris.

The Powerful Queen Kaʻahu-manu

During the time the Big Island's Ka-la-niʻōpuʻu held the Hāna Coast, Ka-hekili was indirectly responsible for one of Hāna's major contributions to Hawaiʻi—the birth of the great Hawaiian chiefess Kaʻahu-manu.

Ka-hekili bested the ruler of Molokaʻi, Keʻeaumoku, who with his wife sought refuge in Hāna. A girl, Kaʻahu-manu, was born to them in a cave in the side of Ka-ʻuiki in 1768.

Battles between Ka-hekili and Ka-laniʻōpuʻu swept past the very door of Keʻeaumoku's exile home in Hāna in the next several years. During the protracted skirmishing on the Hāna Coast, Ka-laniʻōpuʻu drew on the help of soldiers and priests from Oʻahu, including a widely respected prophet. On a visit to Hāna, the prophet told Kaʻahu-manu, then a child of 10, that she would be loved by a chief and would become the wife of a king. While he declined to give the men's names, he told her father that he would play a part in the drama and would die in peace. And so

it came to pass.

Keʻeaumoku played a pivotal role in the Big Island battle which made Ka-mehameha master of Kona, Kohala and Hāmākua, the base from which the warrior eventually went on to rule all of the islands.

When Ka-mehameha was engaged in peaceful pursuits on the Big Island and Kaʻahu-manu was an attractive young woman of 17, her father introduced her to the royal Hawaiian court. She attracted the immediate attention of the king. While there was little in the rugged appearance of the king to attract her, Kaʻahu-manu was ambitious. And so, with admiration, if no affection for the great King Ka-mehameha, she consented to become his wife.

Kaʻahu-manu was the king's third wife, but she was by no means just one more woman in the king's court. She was a strong-willed individual. She took a lover even though Ka-mehameha had placed a *kapu* on her body.

When he found this out, he banished her from court, although the two were re-united through the peacemaking efforts of Capt. George Vancouver.

Before Ka-mehameha's death in 1819, he named Kaʻahu-manu *kuhina nui,* queen regent, making her a joint ruler with his son Liholiho.

Kaʻahu-manu wasted no time in exercising her power. At King Liholiho's coronation Kaʻahu-manu and her retinue regally strode to center position in the longhouse. Over her *pāʻū* of yellow satin she wore Ka-mehameha's royal feather cloak and in her right hand she carried the king's ceremonial spear. And she stood, imperious and commanding, awaiting the arrival of Liholiho.

Later that same year, Kaʻahu-manu assured her place in the history of Hawaiʻi by destroying the *kapu* system that had been the foundation of the Hawaiian religious/political order. At a public feast she ate with men and ate food forbidden to women—two ancient *kapu* broken.

Shortly after this, she opened the way for Christianity in the islands. Initially she simply tolerated the missionaries, who arrived the year after she took control. Later she became their zealous convert. She and the Reverend William Richards wrote the first laws of the new Hawaiian nation, basing them on Moses' Ten Commandments.

When Kaʻahu-manu died, just before dawn on June 5, 1832, in Oʻahu's Mānoa Valley, she was holding a copy of a newly printed copy of the *New Testament* in Hawaiian that the Reverend Hiram Bingham had given her.

The birth and life of this great Hawaiian leader is marked on Ka-ʻuiki each year in August by the people of the Hāna Coast, with a solemn re-creation of the investiture of the queen-to-be.

—R. Y.

the Hāna Coast continued much as it had for centuries.

As the population began to increase, a few centuries after the initial settlement, the presence of people began to have an impact on the *ʻāina,* the land. By 1200 A.D. the more marginal lands were permanently settled, and by 1400 A.D. forests were replaced by cultivated fields and valley basins were converted to vast irrigation systems.

The increasing population also led to greater social complexity, and a feudal system of land management evolved, with each island headed by at least one *mōʻī,* or king. The best lands were reserved for the king. The rest were allotted to warrior chiefs who, in turn, gave direct control of some lands to their most faithful followers, and so on, with the divisions of land becoming smaller and the lowest portion going to the common people.

The largest geographic subdivision on each island was known as a *moku.* The Hāna area, from Ke-ʻanae to Kau-pō, made up one *moku.*

Each *moku* was divided into *ahupuaʻa,* and each of these was ruled by a chief. Although there were exceptions, an *ahupuaʻa* was a wedge-shaped parcel of land, with its widest part on the shore and its point at the highest elevation of land, giving the governing chief access to the resources of the mountain, the plain and the sea. *Ahupuaʻa* ranged in size from a few hundred acres to more than 100,000 acres; many in the Hāna area are still marked on U.S. government maps.

The *ahupuaʻa* was divided into *ʻili.* Some *ʻili* were the property of the chief holding the *ahupuaʻa;* others belonged to the king.

Parts of the *ʻili* that could be cultivated were divided into *moʻo,* which were then subdivided into smaller tracts called *paukū.*

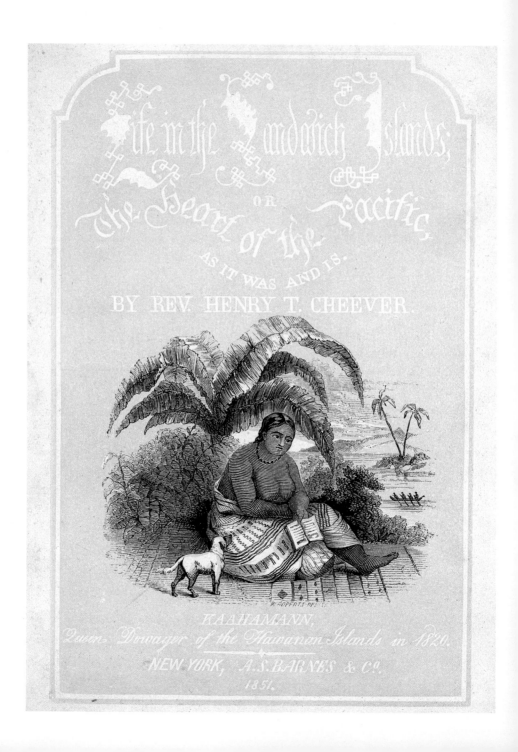

Life in the Sandwich Islands;
OR
The Heart of the Pacific,
AS IT WAS AND IS.

BY REV. HENRY T. CHEEVER.

KAAHAMANN,
Queen Dowager of the Hawaiian Islands in 1820.

NEW YORK, A.S. BARNES & Cº.
1851.

Church interior, Kau-pō.

KA MANAOIO KA MANAOLANA A ME KEALOHA KEALOHA NO NAE KAI OI AE

IF YE SEEK ME   YE SHALL FIND ME

Land cultivated for the chiefs by the common people were called *kō'ele*. The smallest land unit was cultivated for a single family and was known as a *kīhāpai.*

In many respects, the individual Hawaiian found himself in a situation analogous to a European serf, with one big difference: The Hawaiians were free to move from the land of one chief to the land of another. This freedom of movement made for charismatic leaders. As the *ali'i* collected taxes from the people living on their land, they depended on the support of their people to further any personal ambitions.

The freedom of movement was made essential by the agricultural methods used. Like tropical agriculturalists everywhere, the Hawaiians made extensive use of one great tool: fire. Tracts of forest or bush were cleared and burned to create garden plots. After several years of cultivation these were abandoned to secondary vegetation, and new plots were cleared.

The basic concept of early land management practiced by the Hawaiians has been termed a form of stewardship. The land a person farmed belonged to someone else, but was under the farmer's control as long as he occupied it. This concept would have great importance in the development of the Hāna Coast in modern times.

In 1840 King Ka-mehameha III declared that the land belonged to both the chiefs and the people in common, which meant that those who worked a piece of land could not be driven off by the king or the chiefs.

In 1845, a commission was established to determine land rights, no easy task considering that there were no mathematic surveys and that proof of ownership was handed down by word of mouth.

However, the commission in three years processed more than 12,000 individual claims, resulting in the "Great Mahele" of 1848. *Māhele* means "division." The commission recommended that all the land be divided into three equally valuable parts: a

New shoes and bare feet: a 1912 railroad gang.

third to the crown, a third to the chiefs and a third to the common people.

Ka-mehameha III signed the first *māhele* on Jan. 27, 1848, and the final one about two months later. Each *māhele* was recorded in a huge volume called *The Mahele Book*.

Individual claims had to be presented to the land commission and a commutation fee paid to the government before free and clear title was granted. For Hawaiian families working their *kīhāpai,* this was a burden. It is not known how many of the Hawaiians simply failed to make claims or even knew that claims had to be made, but many just continued living as their fathers and their fathers had.

It was a loose arrangement, as most transition systems are, and it enabled the more crafty and/or informed to acquire land cheaply and easily. Thus the Hawaiians of the Hāna Coast, who had known so many masters through the centuries, fell under the sway of new masters. Like the old,

these new masters claimed control over the land. Like the old, the new masters required work. But where the old had ruled by the power of birthright and personal charisma, the new masters ruled with paper.

Much of the power went to the new sugar industry.

The first sugar operation in the Hāna area was begun by George Wilfong, a *haole* sea captain, who settled there at a time when Maui, and the rest of the islands, did a booming business replenishing stores for the more than 1,500 whaling ships then plying the north Pacific. In 1849, when gold was found at Sutter's Mill in California, the resulting flood of greedy humanity created a pricey market for any and all commodities, including sugar, that could be shipped out of Hawai'i. Seeking to capitalize on this boom, Wilfong set himself up in business with 60 acres of cane land and a mill near Ka-'uiki.

He appears to have been a hard-headed

Visitors to a Hawaiian home in Kī-pahulu, 1904.

entrepreneur, cast in the mold of most of the sea captains of the time—someone who looked at human beings as belonging to one of two groups: those who owned and those who worked at the pleasure of those who owned.

Although he apparently stopped short of dragooning field and mill workers, his methods of dealing with the resident population were, at best, opportunistic.

Wilfong bound his workers to 10-year contracts, offering them $150 cash up front and then setting up a company store to get the money back. It was the first taste of the industrial age on the Hāna Coast, one that must have been as bitter as the cane, first brought to these shores by the Polynesians, was sweet.

It is not known if the workers understood the terms of the contract or if they realized before signing it that they were no longer free to move on if they felt like it. But it was apparent, both in Hāna and elsewhere, that once the Hawaiians knew the score, they became unwilling plantation workers. These proud people had experienced too much individual freedom to be yoked to some clock ticking away above a set of ledgers.

The first Chinese laborers were imported to Hāna in 1852. More accustomed to the conditions of contract labor, the Chinese made short-term commitments (usually three years) and as soon as these were fulfilled moved out on their own to set up small farms or merchant enterprises.

Once the California Gold Rush settled down and the premium prices for Hawaiian commodities dropped, Wilfong's mill burned down. In light of his reputed labor-management practices, arson could be suspected.

It remained for two Danish brothers to firmly establish sugar as a new economic center on the Hāna Coast. In 1864, August and Oscar Unna raised $47,000 to start what eventually would become the Hāna Plantation.

Four years later, the first Japanese laborers, mostly bachelor second sons expecting to earn some money and then return home, arrived in Hāna holding three-year contracts signed with an organization that would become known later as the Hawaiian Sugar Planters Association.

The brothers Unna were among the founders of the association, which acted as lobbyist and over-all administrator for the sugar owners/growers, just as it does today.

Twelve years after the Unnas set up their plantation, King Ka-lā-kaua negotiated the Sugar Reciprocity Treaty with the United States.

This "give and take" treaty gave favored status to the Kingdom of Hawaiʻi and, most importantly for the sugar growers, did away with a two-cent-a-pound U.S. tariff on Hawaiian sugar. That made the island sweetener competitive on the mainland market.

The treaty was just the sort of thing awaited by those foreigners who had been busily acquiring land since the Great Mahele.

When planters could not obtain land outright, through whatever means, they often resorted to leasing acreage. The idea of leasing land was compatible with the previous concept of land stewardship, but the problem, which would continue to haunt land cases on the Hāna Coast for more than a century, was remembering who leased what from whom, and for how long.

In the early 1900s there was a great deal of wheeling and dealing in land on the Hāna Coast as smaller sugar plantations came and went, usually to be consolidated into bigger operations. The land leases were considered assets and, as such, were included in the negotiations.

A further complication was caused by the shrinking of the native Hawaiian population due to disease and wanderlust.

All of this resulted in a muddle that is

still causing problems as 100-year-old land claims are re-asserted by descendants and relatives who have lived on other islands and in other places for generations.

At the turn of the 20th Century, sugar plantations proliferated on the Hāna Coast, mostly in the area right around Hāna itself. Other, more exotic agricultural ventures took place in the outlying areas of the district, including attempts at commercial cultivation of rubber (Nā-hiku), wheat (Kau-pō), and tobacco (ʻUlu-pala-kua). The area even had a brief brush with pineapple. The Haiku Fruit and Packing Co. in 1922 planted pineapple in Mūʻolea, in the Kī-pahulu area, and in 1924 built a cannery in Hāna Town itself. The venture was given up as an economic fiasco in 1927, and the pineapple cannery in Hāna Town is now a ruin.

Generally, the Hāna Coast is known for sugar. By 1883, there were six separate sugar plantations on the Hāna Coast— Kaeleku Sugar Co., Hamoa Agricultural

Rubber tree tapping, Nā-hiku.

Co., Kawaipapa Agricultural Co., Hāna Sugar Co., Reciprocity Sugar Co., and Haneoo Agricultural Co. Both the Hamoa and Haneoo companies were absorbed later by Kaeleku Co., a C. Brewer holding.

While the sugar industry on the Hāna Coast had its economic ups and downs, for the plantation worker it was all a downward spiral. The Hawaiian Sugar Planters Association, in league with royal and later territorial governments, kept a lid on labor costs by the simple expedient of importing workers from all over the world.

The Chinese and Japanese were followed by the Portuguese from the Azores, Puerto Ricans, Spaniards, Filipinos and others, all installed in plantation camps where the lord and master was the plantation manager. Orders were carried out by an ethnic hodge-podge of *luna,* supervisors, imported from Denmark, Scotland, Germany and the United States.

Life on the Hāna Coast was probably better for the imported workers than it had been "back home," but it was hard. In 1900 the average pay for plantation workers was $15 a month for 26 days of work, 10 hours a day in the field or 12 in the mill—computing to less than five cents an hour. There was partial compensation in the form of housing, rudimentary schooling for children, some medical care, recreation programs—the plantation supplied it all, but at a price.

By 1942 the average annual wage for a sugar plantation worker on Oʻahu was $928, but workers on the Hāna Coast earned from one-half to two-thirds less, or less than $500 a year.

The plantation workers augmented their incomes in time-honored ways—by fishing, hunting, raising their own food. Economic necessity led many of the foreign-born plantation workers into adopting life styles not much different than the earlier Hawaiians, life styles that persist today, lending a stability to the socio-economic rhythms of the Hāna Coast.

Hāna travelers of the 1880s call on Mr. A. Unna: (from left)
Mr. O. Unna, Judge Fornander, Gov. Dominis, Mr. C. Brown,
Mrs. Sheldon, Princess Liliuokalani, Mr. A. Unna,
Capt. Toomey, Mrs. A. Unna, and Mrs. Hedemann.

CHRISTIAN HEDEMANN

In early 1878 August Unna made the long and arduous voyage back to Denmark, his homeland, expressly to find an engineer to supervise the construction of equipment for the new sugar mill in Hāna. He recruited the young Christian Jacob Hedemann, who left with his bride for the Sandwich Islands, as they were then known, on May 3 of that year. The newlyweds were both 25.

Fortunately for those who later would be interested in knowing firsthand what the Hāna Coast was like at that time, Christian Hedemann took up photography as a way to entertain himself in his new home.

Their journey from Denmark took them across the U.S. by train and across the Pacific Ocean by steamer. They departed Honolulu bound for Hāna on June 27 aboard a small packet boat with no cabins except one that was reserved for the captain. The rough crossing of the Moloka'i Channel left Meta Hedemann too seasick and weak to walk up the hill from Hāna Bay to her new home. In her journal, she describes her arrival this way:

There was quite a walk from the landing up to the house where they lived and where we were to stay until we could get a bungalow for ourselves, and as I was quite weak and exhausted from the terrible sea trip, the men decided to send a cart drawn by a pair of oxen for me. In this they placed a "rocking chair" for me to sit in, and in such "style" I made my entrance to the wonderful Hana plantation! I do not know which was the most awful, the sea trip or that ride in the cart up the hill to the house, the rocking chair, the two fat, lumbering bullocks and the bumpy road.

Not long after this auspicious arrival, Hāna was visited by King Ka-lā-kaua, who kept a cottage nearby. The king and his considerable retinue spent the night at the Unna's home, where His Majesty's private cook oversaw the preparation of a sumptuous meal.

Kalakaua carved the immense turkey, asking me which part of the bird I preferred, and in every way I was served first. The king spoke perfect English, and acted in all ways as a high class white gentleman . . .

The weather at Hāna was considerably different than either of the Hedemanns had experienced before.

One day I remember we had a terrific shower. It came down like a big waterfall on the side of the hills. That morning the old Hawaiian man who brought milk up to our house in a little tin bucket appeared in the kitchen without a stitch of clothing on . . . just as naked as the day he was born . . . with the exception of wearing a hat. Water dripped from his brown body, and laughing and chatting to me he finally took off his hat to show me that his pants and shirt were stuffed inside, so that when the rain stopped he would have dry clothes to put on . . .

In 1884 Hedemann and his wife moved to Honolulu, taking, of course, his camera with them. The following year he and 50 other amateur photographers formed the Hawaiian Camera Club, and during the next several years these early club members produced numerous photographic exhibits, lantern slide shows and thousands of pictures of 19th Century Hawai'i. The club's success was attributed largely to Hedemann's energetic leadership.

On the preceeding and following pages is a selection of photographs taken by Hedemann on, and of, the Hāna Coast.

Hawaiian family at Hāna: a formal portrait.

The cane mill at Hāna

The vacuum pan at Hāna.

Overview of late 19th Century Hāna; note
Wananalua Church, upper right.

A grass house that once stood at the site of today's
Hana Kai Resort.

Hāna, 1891.

CHAPTER III

INTO HANA'S 20TH CENTURY
WITH SHIPS, SUGAR AND A VISITOR INDUSTRY

Through most of the 20th Century, the main link
between the Hāna Coast and "Out There" was the sea.
Many old stone foot highways had been overgrown,
plowed under or quarried for other building projects.

chooners and later steamers
running between the islands
made regular calls to drop off
supplies and pick up cargo,
including the all important
sugar. The steamers which stopped at Ke-
'anae, Nā-hiku, Hāna, Kī-pahulu, Kau-pō
and Nu'u also brought the coast's first va-
cationing visitors.

A rather narrow glimpse of Hāna in the
early days of this century is provided by
Honolulu newspaper accounts. In the Sep-
tember 3, 1910, issue of *The Pacific Commercial Advertiser* (predecessor to today's
Honolulu Advertiser) there is an article
about the arrival of a group of travelers on
the SS *Claudine* at Hāna:

> . . . while the landing is all right
> for freight, it is mightily inconven-
> ient for passengers and when the
> swell is heavy it must be dangerous
> to life and limb. Passengers leaving
> here have to jump into the arms of
> the boat boys, and on occasion have
> to be grabbed and thrown from the
> boat to the wharf.
> The visitor to Hāna puts up at the
> comfortable club maintained by
> L. Y. Aiona, a Chinese gentleman of
> parts who runs the club rather as an
> accommodation for visitors than as a
> money-making proposition. A man
> at the house of whom every visitor to

Hāna calls is W. P. Haia, the Bismark
of the Maui County Board of Supervisors.

The account in the newspaper credits
one C. O. Cooper with being the mayor of
Hāna, probably an honorary title. The reporter notes that Cooper maintained a nursery of young trees and whenever a digni-
tary arrived in Hāna, Cooper had them
plant a tree on Ka 'uiki.

The account also notes the police department had 10 men under the supervi-
sion of a deputy sheriff, Levi L. Joseph,
who "has at present just caught a counter-
feiter!"

It was during this time that a son of Hāna
embarked on a career in classical opera.
Tandy MacKenzie, born in Hāna in 1892
and graduated from Kamehameha Schools
in Honolulu in 1912, was hailed by critics
and conductors as the world's greatest living operatic tenor, not just a worthy successor to Caruso but superior to him.

German music fans greeted his 1929 de-
but in Munich with 31 curtain calls, nearly
an hour of applause, and proceeded to
carry him through the streets on their
shoulders. MacKenzie was the headliner at
the opening of the New Memorial Opera
House in San Francisco in 1932 and in the
mid 1930s drew accolades from more than
20,000 persons a night at the Hollywood
Bowl.

MacKenzie is considered by many to be the most highly esteemed and acclaimed Hawaiian performer in history. His opera career spanned 1929–1954. Though his career never came to full flower, for a variety of personal and financial reasons, his artistic achievements were unimpeachable.

The early years of the 20th Century were a time of growth and increasing prosperity on the Hāna Coast. This development continued steadily through the 1930s when the area reached its peak population of about 3,500 persons.

A major event of this period was the completion of the road to "Out There." In 1877, a road was constructed from Central Maui to Kai-lua in order to build the Hāmākua Ditch. Roads existed from Hāna to Ke-'anae from ancient times. But it wasn't until 1926 that the Territorial Government shipped in a gang of prison trusties, established them in a camp at Ke-'anae, and turned barely passable foot and mule trails between Ke-'anae and Kai-lua into a cinder-paved highway that could handle trucks and cars.

When the road was opened the next year, it was a big event in Hāna, with a parade and a two-day lū'au for the first motorists who made the 55-mile drive in from Wai-luku.

Keeping the road open was another story. The territorial and, later, state departments of transportation became major employers, supplying the cash-jobs residents needed to augment their subsistent life styles. During the winter rains, the road was often victimized by mud slides, rock falls, downed trees and flood erosion.

As long as the sugar plantations held sway on the Hāna Coast, most people traveled by foot, just as their Hawaiian predecessors had done. Every village was within walking distance of churches, stores, schools and whatever jobs were available. And if something wasn't within walking distance, the folks of the coast just didn't go, unless it was to Lahaina or O'ahu for high school. The schools on the Hāna Coast stopped at the eighth grade, so an eighth grade education was the norm. Only a few went away to school. It was common for children as young as 12 to go to work in the fields, chopping weeds.

Nearly everything was done by hand on the plantations, from the plowing (with bullock teams) to the planting to the cutting and carrying of the heavy stalks to the sugar trains for transport to the mills.

Until 1937 sugar cane was moved from the main fields to the mills via railroad. Workers laid temporary track in the fields to connect them with the more permanent lines. The trains were abandoned in favor of trucks on the grounds that the trucks would be more economical.

During the 1920s and 1930s, Hāna was a bustling place. There was a choice of two movie theaters (and had been since 1919) with one at Ka-'elekū, near where the current airport is located, and the other in Hāna Town itself. Besides Hāna Town and Ka-'elekū there were self-sufficient villages at Ke-'anae, Nā-hiku, Kī-pahulu and Kau-pō—each with its Soon General Store, school and choice of Protestant or Roman Catholic church. Hāna Town was the hub, with fifteen different stores, three barbershops, a pool hall, a choice of several restaurants and two shows a night at the movie house, which also had Saturday matinees.

In 1934 the old prison road-gang camp at Ke-'anae became home for the Hāna Coast's Civilian Conservation Corps, one of Franklin D. Roosevelt's job programs designed to combat the effects of the Depression. The CCC provided jobs for islanders from other areas of the state, fi-

Tandy MacKenzie as Canio in the opera *I Pagliacci*.

Angry waters in Hāna Bay following the destructive
tidal wave of '46.

nancing the planting of thousands of eucalyptus and assorted other trees on the upper slopes above Hāna as well as the mantle of ironwood trees on Ka-'uiki.

Another Roosevelt instituted make-work agency, named the Works Progress Administration (WPA), also made itself felt on the Hāna Coast during the 1930s by financing a motor road through from Kī-pahulu to Kau-pō on the backside of the island.

The normally tranquil Hāna weather has a knack for occasionally reminding residents that there are more powerful forces than man. A severe drought hit the area in 1924, resulting in water rations and a residential outcry for water system improvements—an appeal that was repeated at intervals until the late 1970s, when the state sank two wells for drinking water in the Hāna area.

Nature again made herself known in 1938, when an earthquake with its epicen-ter in the 'Ale-nui-hāhā Channel rattled everything and everyone on the Hāna Coast. The quake, as reported in *The Honolulu Star-Bulletin,* shattered two Standard Oil tanks, dumping 30,000 gallons of petro-chemicals into the sea; razed water tanks and stone walls, caving in one church completely; covered both the Ha'i-kū/Hāna and Kau-pō/Kī-pahulu roads with landslides; and destroyed enough of the Ka-'elekū plantation power plant to cause a three-day blackout. Miraculously, no one was hurt.

The most monumental natural disaster to hit the Hāna Coast came April 1, 1946, from the sea itself. It began at 1:59 a.m. (Hawai'i time) when the crust of the earth shivered in the Aleutian Islands on the northern rim of the Pacific. That shiver sent waves coursing toward Hawai'i at almost five hundred miles an hour.

Nothing stood between the Hāna Coast and the onslaught, which arrived at about 6:30 a.m.—towering waves crunching

One of Hāna's first automobiles, 1922.

against the shore in a succession of sledge-hammer blows.

The Ke-'anae Peninsula was nearly swept clean; only the old stone church remained standing. Hāmoa was obliterated. Whole villages along the coast disappeared. The massive *tsunami,* tidal wave, hit all of the islands that fateful April Fool's Day morning, but the toll in human life was the heaviest on Maui along the Hāna Coast.

As the day moved to a conclusion, the people of Hāna searched through the rubble, hoping against hope. Many families were reunited with tears of relief in their eyes. For others, the tears came from grief.

The dead:

Walter Handy, 89, Ke-'anae; Mrs. Helen Tau-a, 48, Ke-'anae; Mrs. Mary Kahula, 50, Hāna; Mrs. Mary Anne Dusson, 65, Hāna; Gisaku Idemoto, 80, Lower Pā'ia; Robert Cullen, 3 months, Hāna; Richard Atay, 6 months, Hāna; Kenneth Atay, 4, Hāna; Junior Mendez, 3, Hāna.

The missing:

Paul Atay, 2, Hāna; Leroy Mendez, 1½, Hāna; Patricia Mendez, 2½, Hāna.

The mortally injured:

Mrs. Elizabeth Mendez, Hāna.

April 1, 1946, will be remembered on the Hāna Coast as the day the sea came and took loved ones away.

While World War II was still over the horizon, at least one enlightened bureaucrat saw it coming a full six months before Pearl Harbor.

Leslie Medeiros, a policeman in Hāna for more than 33 years, was part of the five-man force in 1941 when an order came out to train a squad of provisional policemen, a para-military group of volunteers. "No one explained why; just said to do it," Medeiros recalls.

The 21 provisional police officers were trained in observation techniques and military maneuvers and were armed. They weren't needed for active defense, then

Joe and Annie Kahaleuahi.

Storm at Hāna

Lying as she does, abruptly open to the sea on one side and with her great gullies and gorges roaring up the cliffs to the lip of Hale-a-ka-lā on the other, the Hāna Coast is often mistress to storms of sudden fury and to heavy mountain rains that can quickly change streams and rivulets into booming, uncontrollable furies of water. Hāna people are the children of a land filled with beauty and generously bountiful in the myriad things she provides. They say of her, *"Ku'u 'umeke pākākā"*, "my large calabash". But they know well that in balance they are the children of a parent sometimes possessed of fearsome, unreasoned anger, and they live their lives in accordance with this natural and wild disorder.

On March 30, 1982, a storm roared into Hāna from the northwest, its winds cracking great trees and toppling power and telephone lines in more than three hundred places. Massive landslides covered the road above Ke-'anae and literally destroyed it at Kau-pō, where the stream tore at the earth and stone until it was reduced to a level fully 15 feet below that which had existed before.

Dozens of huge, uprooted trees swirled in the turbulent mud-brown waters of usually tranquil Hāna Bay.

The airport was flooded and closed. While the storm continued unabated, officials estimated that Hāna would be isolated and without power for seven days or more.

In the darkness of late afternoon, Hana Ranch headquarters was quickly surrounded by a wide assortment of off-road vehicles, most of them equipped with Citizens Band radios. Winches, lengths of strong rope and chain saws were much in evidence, their presence eerily reflected in the revolving blue light of a police cruiser. Coleman lanterns illuminated yellow-slickered figures moving about inside the office as the men gathered to exchange informa-

tion and assurances, and to assimilate plans for the safety and comfort of Hāna's people.

Of immediate concern was an adequate food supply and the fact that the contents of well-provisioned freezers would soon thaw and spoil without electricity.

Those men who owned gasoline-powered generators gathered at one side of the room, tracing a grid of the town and its surroundings with their fingers as they talked. A plan was devised providing for volunteers to move the generators around on changing shifts to provide temporary power to homes with freezers on a rotating basis.

Later a few lights flickered through the rain, and through an open window one of the volunteers could be seen sitting with a man and his wife at their kitchen table. The men were drinking beer and the three of them were laughing.

—**Carl Lindquist**

or later when a company of regular Army soldiers from Tennessee were stationed at Hāmoa.

The Hāna Coast's closest brush with the shooting war came very early. On January 28, 1942, the small transport *Gen. Royal T. Frank* was negotiating the 'Ale-nui-hāhā Channel when it was torpedoed by a submarine of the Imperial Japanese Navy. Luckily for those who survived the explosions and fire on the little transport, the interisland tug *Kalae* was nearby, and the skipper maneuvered his small boat and large barge around to pick up survivors. Twenty-nine died during the initial attack, but all the others were saved. The *Kalae* and her barge brought the survivors into Hāna Town, where the community turned out to help the victims, many of whom were badly burned. The Hāna School gymnasium was turned into an emergency hospital under the command of the district's only physician, Dr. Frank St. Sure Jr.

"We didn't lose a one of the men brought in, although some were very badly burned," Medeiros said with a pride that survived the 41 intervening years.

The provisional police were put to work in observation posts scattered from Ke-'anae to Kau-pō and linked by field telephone to Hāna's police station. The volunteers worked 12-hour shifts and, at night, listened for the sound of submarines coming to the surface to recharge their batteries.

For the new police commander, a sergeant with six months' experience on the force, the process of registering all Hāna district residents—on orders from military commanders at Pearl Harbor—was a romantic event. In organizing the volunteer registrars, Sgt. Hannibal Tavares met and fell in love with Harriet Yoshiye Tanaka, whom he hired as a secretary once registration was finished. Soon after, the Makawao boy and the Hāna girl began a marriage that Tavares credits as the most

The lava stone memorial to Paul I. Fagan atop "Lyon's Hill."

The Hāna Seals and their patron, Paul Fagan (upper left).

important ingredient in a career that took him from the police station at Hāna to the executive suites of Alexander & Baldwin to the office of mayor of Maui County.

Tavares' fondness for Hāna extends beyond his wife. His two daughters were born in Hāna, and, as he expansively adds, "Hāna is *lūʻau* country."

As the war moved farther away, it was apparent that the day of small volume, labor-intensive sugar production was a thing of the past.

The International Longshoremen and Warehouse Workers Union—better known as the ILWU—was making strides in unionizing the sugar workers.

C. Brewer officials feared that the Hāna operation could not support the wage demands being raised. Rather than run the risk of antagonizing the union, which might have retaliated against other sugar operations, the company decided to close down the Kaeleku Plantation and take

whatever capital gain could be realized from the sale of the property.

Thus in 1946 hundreds of plantation workers found their jobs gone, and, with their jobs, their plantation-supplied housing and their very way of life.

The hero in this scene was Paul I. Fagan, a hard-charging entrepreneur from San Francisco who had acquired the Hana Sugar Co. from the Unna brothers in the 1930s. Fagan had left his investment pretty much alone until the mid 1940s, when he decided that Hāna would be the place to which he retired.

At that time, Hāna's hillsides were covered with sugar cane, and the town had the dusty frontier feeling of all plantation villages, with cane trucks rumbling through the streets, spreading a spoor of dust and cane stalk shards. There had been technological advances in sugar production, but it was clear to Fagan that there was little future for sugar in an area where hand labor was required and volume was low.

Luʻau Time In Hāna

When you're in Hāna, you are indeed in *lūʻau* country.

In fact, there are so many *lūʻau* in Hāna that throwing one has become a communal art form. At the slightest provocation the bamboo guys head for the mountains to cut poles from which the *lūʻau* house will be made, the fishermen grab their nets and go fishing, the *ʻopihi* pickers go off to their secret picking spots, the *laulau* crew begins wrapping ti leaf pouches filled with beef and fish and *lūʻau* leaves, and throughout the community pots of all sizes and description are set to bubbling with the myriad delicacies that go into the culinary potpourri which constitutes a contemporary Hāna *lūʻau*.

The first thing you need to throw a *lūʻau* in Hāna is a good reason. If you don't have a good reason, however, it is perfectly acceptable to make one up. Oh sure, there are *lūʻau* for engagements, weddings, graduations, birthdays, anniversaries, and housewarmings, but everybody has a *lūʻau* for important occasions like these. It's the in-between times that call for really creative thinking.

In Hāna no one would look twice if you threw a *lūʻau* because you got a new job (or just lost an old one), your favorite hunting dog just had pups, you finished painting your house, bought a new boat, were leaving on a trip, or just getting back from one. It is even rumored that every once in a while somebody hosts a *lūʻau* just because they feel like having one, but nobody ever talks about such things.

There are generally two sets of people immediately recognizable at a Hāna *lūʻau*, both given to sitting around and smiling a lot.

The first are the guests of honor, who are so weighted down with leis and food as to be rendered temporarily immobile.

The second is the *imu* gang, also generally immobile, but for a different reason.

These are the hardy souls charged with catching, slaughtering, cleaning, shaving and

Hukilau at Hāna Bay, 1921.

cooking the understandably recalcitrant porker who is destined to become the main course and, as if that weren't enough, with digging the hole, building the fire, heating the stones, cooking the pig and drinking beer. The latter two activities go on all night long, and by *lūʻau* time the pig and the *imu* gang are usually both done to a fare-thee-well.

Hāna *lūʻau* throwers are in unfettered abundance at the New Year—before, during and after the emergence of the new annum.

The New Year's Eve celebration is particularly gala, featuring a lavish fireworks display sponsored by the Hotel Hana-Maui, followed by "da kine" parade which really should be seen from the air to be fully appreciated.

Since fireworks are sent aloft from the hillside directly opposite the hotel entrance, cars and trucks full of revelers line both sides of the street there, with massive quantities of beer, champagne and firecrackers in full evidence.

Precisely at midnight a fusillade of fire-works explodes in a kind of orgasmic frenzy, and the parade of automobiles begins.

To the uninitiated, two factors set this parade apart from any other they have ever witnessed.

First, most of the "floats" aren't; they are ordinary cars and trucks crammed to capacity with yelling, clapping, whistling, honking celebrants.

Second, the parade starts off in two directions at the same time. To make matters even worse, within minutes this duality of direction becomes even more complex as vehicles peel off in twos and threes, heading down various side streets like groups of newly independent amoebae.

Partygoers stand in front of every *lūʻau* site, wildly cheering the now segmented parade on, and the sound of small groups of honking cars passing by goes on well into the birth of a new Hāna day.

—Carl Lindquist

Fagan foresaw the economic dislocation in Hāna and, more important, he did something about it.

It is said that he personally went to the giant Alexander & Baldwin plantation in central Maui and persuaded personnel officials to hire displaced Hana Plantation workers, many of them Filipinos who had come to Maui during the plantation boom days of the 1930s.

And beyond this, Fagan established a viable alternative economic base for the Hāna Coast. Fagan looked at the fields of sugar cane and envisioned pastures dotted with fat beef cattle. In 1944, he decided to pursue that dream, and, abandoning a cattle ranch on the east end of Moloka'i, he acquired 14,000 acres of land in and around Hāna. The white-faced Herefords that have become such an integral part of the scenery at Hāna were shipped from Moloka'i.

Even as he had the former cane fields planted with pangola range grass for his cattle, Fagan saw one more way to utilize the human and geographic resources of Hāna—a visitor industry.

Hawai'i had played host to millions of Americans during the war years but the idea of a visitor industry—a concept invented by the Swiss, another people who lived in a beautiful but isolated and resource-poor area—was little more than a faint ripple outside of Honolulu's Wai-kīkī.

Fagan saw tourism as a way of supplying jobs and cash, for if there was paternalism mixed in with Fagan's dream for Hāna, that paternalism had the hard edge of reality. If Hāna was to survive as a community, there had to be jobs—more jobs than the 20 or so that the Hana Ranch could provide.

So, characteristically, at the same time he was getting the ranch underway and taking over the diesel plant which supplied the town with its lights and power, the re-

doubtable Fagan and his wife, Helene Irwin Fagan, set about to build one of the first resorts in the islands outside of Wai-kīkī. In so doing they guaranteed the continuance of the one constant that has existed throughout the history of the Hāna Coast—its steady stream of visitors.

Before World War II, the occasional visitor to the Hāna Coast had the choice of driving in from central Maui via the unpaved Hāna Highway; coming in by sea on one of the interisland steamers; or, later, flying in on a twin-engine Inter-Island Airways plane. Inter-Island, which would mature into the current day Hawaiian Airlines, used a grassy plain at Hāmoa as a flag stop.

With enormous capital at their disposal, Fagan and his wife had a wide choice of locations for the hotel they envisioned. Building it at Hāmoa, near the area's best beach and close to the grass strip "airport" seemed to some to be the best alternative, but Helene Fagan disagreed. She wanted the hotel closer to the heart of Hāna Town. Her view prevailed, and construction of what was then called the Kauiki Inn was begun.

The hotel was designed for first-class travelers. In those days there was no such thing as a cut-rate tour, and people who visited Hāna had to be well-heeled and time wealthy—visitors who tend to want luxury. Fagan and his wife set about to give them just that.

By October, 1946, Fagan's dream had become what was called in press accounts that "glamorous new resort on the Hana Coast."

In the early days of the Hotel Hana-Maui Fagan's guests were met at the Hāmoa grass airstrip and driven to the hotel, or they were met at the airport in Central Maui and driven by limousine across the cinder-paved, twisting and turning Hāna Highway.

In order to attract the clientele necessary

The grass airstrip at Hāmoa, 1934.

Members of the Hotel Hana Maui's "family" staff.

The Family Hotel

Fagan created more than a four-star stop for jaded travelers when he created the Hotel Hana-Maui. He created an economic center for Hāna, a way for the community to continue into future generations. Fagan created hope.

In the first 10 years of its existence, the hotel grew from the original 10 cottages, a restaurant and a beer parlor, to a facility that included 50 guest rooms. In that first decade, the hotel exposed 30,000 guests to the charms of the Hāna Coast and provided a unique kind of employment.

The term "family hotel" usually means a hotel that caters to families. While that is true for the Hotel Hana-Maui, particularly during the summer months, the term takes on an entirely different meaning in reference to the hotel's employees.

Mary Estrella, the resident manager of the hotel, began at the beginning, in 1946. A Hāna girl, Estrella had graduated from Hāna High School and then gone on to O'ahu to a business school and work. The hotel made it possible for her to come home. During the years she has been at the hotel, she has seen it change ownership twice, most recently in July 1984 when Hāna Ranch and the Hotel Hana-Maui were purchased by the Rosewood Corporation of Dallas, Texas.

"It is so good to see the hotel being renewed," says Estrella. "The employees here and the guests are like one big family, and our 'house' needed more than just another coat of paint."

More than just another coat of paint, indeed, as Rosewood Hotels completes a $24 million remodeling that has doubled the size of the grounds to nearly 50 abundantly flowered acres, while enlarging the hotel itself to 105 bungalow-style rooms.

The genealogy of many Hāna families is so intertwined with the hotel's employee roster that the two are almost indistinguishable. Take the Helekahi family as an example.

Uncle John Helekahi is one of the hotel's executive chefs. His wife, Lovey, is the assistant

social director, and son Arthur a kitchen worker. Arthur's sister, Mapuana, works in the dining room; his wife, Aileen, works in the kitchen. Lovey's uncle Matthew Kalalau is the manager of the grounds department. "But don't start talking about all the Kalalaus that work here," says Mary. "You'll have to write another book."

Fagan's "retirement project" has blossomed, with the help of the Hāna Coast people, into a visitor industry dream of aloha, a fact concretely documented by the fact that 85 per cent of the hotel's business comes from guests who are returning for the second, third, fourth or fifth time.

Jealously protective of the Hawaiian community spirit that permeates its newest property (others include the Mansion on Turtle Creek, the Crescent Court and the Remington in Texas, and the Bel Air in California), Rosewood Hotels has promised an ambitious restoration of culture as well as buildings, and it looks as if one man's dream has been revitalized.

to make the Hotel Hana-Maui a viable "industry" on the Hāna Coast, Fagan pulled off a promotional venture that would pay long-lasting dividends.

Among his holdings was a baseball team, the San Francisco Seals of the Pacific Coast League. They had to hold spring training somewhere, so why not at Hāna?

In 1946 Fagan not only brought his baseball team into Hāna, he brought a cadre of baseball writers with them, and it was one of these adjective addicted sports writers who is credited with creating the term, "Heavenly Hana."

Dispatches from the sports writers were printed in West Coast papers, announcing to the world-at-large the existence of the new resort.

The payoff—for Fagan the investor and the job-poor residents of the Hāna Coast—would be more than a decade in coming. It would be an arrival that was not universally lauded. In years to come there would be those on the Hāna Coast who would complain about the passage of "the good old days", but they were seldom the people who had lived through them.

Fagan did not confine his efforts to his ranch and hotel. In 1956 he built the Hāna Ranch Center at a cost of $100,000 and provided a new home for a post office, Bank of Hawaii branch, barber shop and a lunch room. He built a community center down at the harbor, at a cost of $100,000, and named it Helene Hall, for his wife. The center was donated to the community and is operated by the county.

A trust fund was set up with money from Helene Irwin Fagan's estate to fund the Hāna Community Association, one of the first organizations of its type on the island and, for years, the body overseeing the recreational needs of Hāna's children.

The people of Hāna showed their appreciation by erecting a stone cross on the top

Sam Pryor of Kī-pahulu.

Sam Pryor: The Lindbergh Connection

Samuel Pryor, a vice president of Pan American Airways, and his wife, Mary Taylor Pryor, retired to Hāna in 1963, creating a private paradise on 100 acres of grassland that rolled from mountain to sea in Ki-pahulu, 11 miles beyond Hāna town. Both are now deceased.

Pryor covered his land with a profusion of flowering trees and shrubs and built an A-frame within a stone's throw of a 100-foot waterfall that ebbs and swells according to the mountain rain. And at the very edge of a cliff above the falls, Pryor decide to construct a blue-tiled gazebo.

This veritable Eden, he populated with family, a constant flow of famous or wealthy friends and a small *coterie* of gibbon apes, which he treated almost like children. On the days when Pryor drove into Hāna Town for lunch at the hotel, he always remembered to bring the apes a treat — for example, a piece of banana bread or maybe a stick of juicy pineapple,

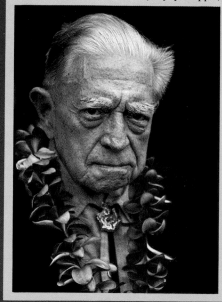

wrapped in a napkin and stuck in a pocket.

Gradually Sam and Mary Tay moved their things from the family home in Darien, Connecticut, to Hāna, and eventually their A-frame was filled, like an old cupboard, with the memorabilia of a life that had taken them from a Sultan's palace in Arabia (where Mary Tay ate with the men and then sat in with the harem) to the original floating markets of Bangkok.

At Pan Am, Pryor had become acquainted with presidents and kings: Lyndon Johnson wrote letters to Hāna from the White House addressed to Mr. Sam, and King Leopold of Belgium sat in the gazebo while Pryor barbecued steaks for dinner. When the king asked if he could help, Mary Tay Pryor put him to work setting the table.

Charles Lindbergh stepped into this idyllic setting as Pryor's friend. They had known each other at Pan Am for years and loved reminiscing about the early days of aviation. Pryor had often urged Lindbergh to stop by Maui, and one day on his way back from a conservation project in the Philippines, the famous flier took him up on it.

Lindbergh drove the whiplash road by jeep with Pryor, making him stop frequently along the way. He was so enchanted by the area that he asked Pryor to find him some land to buy.

Pryor sold him five acres on the ocean, and in 1968 Lindbergh and his wife Anne built a chalet on the cliff above the surf, close enough to hear the waves at night and only a short walk to the Pryors' comfortable A-frame.

Lindbergh spent his last few springs in Hāna, exploring the beaches and mountains, entertaining grandchildren. He loved his home in Kī-pahulu more then any place he'd ever lived. It was here he chose to die.

—Beverly Creamer

Charles Lindbergh's grave, Kī-pahulu.

Roadside fruit stand, Hāna.

of Lyon's Hill, behind the hotel, and dedicating it to the memory of Paul Fagan.

The 1950s were a quiet time on the Hāna Coast. The Hotel Hāna-Maui was still becoming established and in the interim, between the sugar and visitor industries, the population dropped to a modern-day low of 500 persons.

Then the state's paving of the Hāna Highway in 1962 made the road accessible to one-day visitors, people some local residents called "rent-a-car tourists." They were nonetheless welcomed, as they pumped some much needed new cash into Hāna's depressed economy.

By the mid 1960s the funky down-home atmosphere of the Hāna Coast, along with its spectacular natural beauty, began to attract a new kind of visitor—what some oldtimers called "money people"—who came not just to see the place, but to buy land and build homes. The list of names reads like a veritable *Who's Who in the Arts and Industry*. Jim Nabors can be spotted shopping in Hāna Town's only all-purpose store, Richard Pryor has been known to grab a bat in the local baseball games, and George Harrison put a picture of his Hāna home on the cover of his latest album, *Gone Troppo*. But, generally speaking, celebrities on the Hāna Coast maintain a great degree of anonymity, something which is possible for two reasons. First, there is an inborn island courtesy; if you want to disparage someone in Hāna, just call him "pushy." Second, there is a tacit agreement among members of the Maui media to ignore the comings and goings of the famous—something which pleases the celebrity and makes life much more simple for the journalist.

The 1970s were a boom time on Maui, a time when the money flowed, the condominiums and hotels grew and the battle lines were drawn between those who saw the island as a gold mine to be exploited and those who wanted it returned to an agrarian yesterday.

Purdy's Tropical Farms, gone "troppo."

The Hāna Coast was part of that dichotomy.

The county and the state remained major sources of the jobs residents needed to augment their subsistent farming and ranching efforts. Men were anxious to work for the county or state road departments.

The county administration was ruled almost solo by Elmer F. Cravalho, a one-time school teacher who rode to power on a statewide wave of labor union Democrats in the middle 1950s.

The Hāna Coast was run by one of Cravalho's workers, a slight, quiet county agent named Elmer Ching, who struggled with inadequate budgets and hand-me-down equipment to keep operative the antiquated roads and water systems inherited from the plantations.

Mayor Cravalho espoused "quality growth," the same concept evinced in Fagan's development of the Hotel Hana-Maui. This meant going after the wealthiest visitors in an effort to get fewer spending more for a longer time, rather than opening up the floodgates to low-dollar, high-volume tourism.

It was a concept that sat well with the residents of the Hāna Coast.

It seemed possible to keep this isolated coastline a bastion of old-style island life against a veritable siege of changing values. Instead of being the passive recipients of whatever the guys "Out There" decided, the people of the Hāna Coast began taking an active part in their own affairs.

Governmental hearings that were *pro forma* in other parts of the state brought out Hāna residents by the score, and they were not bashful about letting the leaders of government—county, state or federal— know exactly what they wanted.

Helene Hall was the scene of many meetings that saw outside big shots having both their complacency and their plans shattered by the quiet voices of working men and women and their children.

The Death of a Hero—August, 1974

It was hot that month and all along the road beside the cliffs was the sweet, heavy smell of rotting mangoes. The road is lined with giant mango trees, the descendants, some say, of one single mango seed sent from China more than a hundred years before. School children sent for it and, when it arrived, they carefully planted it in the soil of their schoolyard.

Visitors who have never seen mangoes before pick them up gingerly, sniff the oozing sap and taste the stringy flesh. Then they tuck a few away inside their rented cars to savor later, in hotel rooms in Kā'ana-pali or Ka-hu-lui, far away from Hāna.

As the visitors to Hāna that summer marvelled at this lovely place, a drama was unfolding that would within a few years double, triple and quadruple their numbers. In a cottage above the sea, three miles outside of Hāna Town, most of the immediate Lindbergh family had gathered for a final farewell.

When his doctors said they could do nothing more to check the cancer that had begun growing in his lungs, Charles Lindbergh checked out of the New York hospital, and flew secretly to Maui, where he felt he could control the quality of his final days and of his death. Together for the last eight days of his life, he and his family tied up loose ends and planned his funeral to the smallest detail. He wanted to be buried barefoot and he wanted his friends to come in their work clothes.

In the days that were left to him, Lindbergh took part in almost every activity, from his medical care to the design of his coffin. He smiled when he told John Hanchett, the Hana Ranch foreman who was his friend, that it should be wide enough for his broad shoulders.

Daily Lindbergh discussed his weakening condition with his doctor, Milton Howell, the town's sole physician.

Lindbergh designed his own grave—large enough for both he and Anne—and sketched out its pipe drainage system and the way the rocks would be "wedged in" to form the stone sides. Through Hanchett, he supervised its construction, which was done by Hāna cowboys, headed by Tevi Kahaleuahi.

On Lindbergh's diagrams he even sketched the headstone. He was definite about what he wanted: a block of grey Vermont granite large enough not to tempt souvenir hunters. He chose two lines from his favorite *Bible* passage, Psalm 139, cut precisely one-quarter of an inch into the stone: deep enough to see, but shallow enough that the wind and rain could keep them washed clean. They read, " . . . if I take the wings of the morning and dwell in the uttermost parts of the sea . . ."

On the Monday morning he died, August 26, 1974, it was Tevi who lifted Lindbergh's body into the coffin and who stood barefoot in the back of Babes Hanchett's pickup as it carried the rough hewn eucalyptus coffin from the cottage to the Ho'omau Congregational Church in Kī-pahulu.

The procession was simple—a jeep, the doctor's car, a nurse, a policeman. So was the service. Milton Howell's wife, Roselle; his nurse, Sherry; and Helen Pahuwai, who had occasionally cooked and cleaned for the Lindberghs, filled the church with boughs of colorful bougainvillea, stalks of fragrant ginger, and blossoms of hibiscus and plumeria. Charles had wanted nothing special, but Roselle knew that Anne would appreciate it. In the cool silence before the service began, Helen walked barefoot up to the wooden coffin, carrying flowers in her apron. One by one, she scattered them across its surface.

Service station owner Henry Kahula led the singing of *Angel's Welcome*, as Lindbergh was buried in the shade of a small natal plum a few feet from the old Hawaiian graves where he had once cleared underbrush.

—**Beverly Creamer**

Charles Lindbergh and the *Spirit of St. Louis,* just before his
historic trans-Atlantic flight in 1927.

Charles Lindbergh
February 4, 1902–August 26, 1974.

The Hero Hunters

It's hard to pinpoint the day it started. It was all so gradual. First a few cars, then a few more, and then a steady stream of them, challenging the curves of the Hāna Highway and the weight capacity of the old bridges. Rent-a-cars, then mini-buses, then an occasional tour bus that managed incredibly to maneuver its bulk around the road of cutbacks and sheer drops.

The eyes behind the glass stared curiously out at the scenery they passed. Half of them came to see the seven "sacred" pools and the other half to see where the hero was buried. Some of them weren't quite sure which hero. It all blurred together after a while: one more valley, one more name.

A carload stopped Mary Tay Pryor one day to ask, "Do you know where the Wright brothers are buried?"

The numbers doubled in the first year after Lindbergh was buried there. They doubled again the following year and the one af-

ter that and soon there were 400 to 450 people a day asking the rangers at the seven pools where the grave was.

The rangers developed an automatic response. One hand would rise and a finger would point and they'd find themselves saying, "A mile down the road on the left." There was no sign on the road, and they didn't offer any more words of assistance.

Charles Lindbergh was buried next to Ho'omau Congregational Church, Kī-pahulu's first Protestant church, built in 1857.

The Pryors would visit the churchyard a couple of times a week in the first few years after the funeral, to talk to the visitors and check on things. They'd riffle through the guest book, and count 100 signatures on some days.

But they saw other things too. People tracked mud into the church and tossed cigarettes and garbage around. They walked on the graves and picked the flowers. The smooth *'ili'ili* stones, the kind that cover traditional Hawaiian graves, all disappeared in the first couple of years and had to be replaced. Even the offering box cemented into the wall of the church was ripped out by someone hunting a souvenir.

This upset the Pryors so much that they asked Anne Lindbergh to write a short notice to be placed above the church door. It reads:

> May we remind you that this church is a place of worship and the graveyard is consecrated ground. You are welcome to enter the church in a spirit of reverence and to walk quietly in the surrounding paths. We ask you not to step on the graves or disturb the stones or flowers out of respect for the dead and consideration for the feelings of their relatives.

—Beverly Creamer

Ruins of a Hawaiian school at Moku-lau.

Largely cut off from the mass media that helped shape the concepts of other Mauians, the people of the Hāna Coast saw development plans in terms of their own lives.

The controversy over the highway typifies the approach to the future in Hāna.

Until just recently and since it was first paved by the state in 1962, the Hāna Highway had received only haphazard maintenance.

As winter rains and daily traffic battered the thinly paved road, it became a 55-mile nightmare of potholes and nonexistent shoulders. Driving it meant subjecting a vehicle to suspension destroying conditions and a driver to blind curves that frayed nerves and contributed to more than one collision.

The road also brought in one-day tourists—a boon when they were spending money in Hāna Town, a bane when a resident was stuck behind one while trying to get in or out of the coast.

Even though it was hampering their trips to "town" and destroying their vehicles in the process, residents delayed substantive rebuilding of the road for years because they were afraid a major upgrading would result in a tidal wave of visitors and would destroy the fragile balance between being fed by tourism and being consumed by it.

There was periodic talk of creating a toll road, of limiting the highway's use and of other schemes that would have enabled residents to come and go in reasonable fashion and still maintain the isolation Hāna prized.

The conflict was resolved, finally, in 1982 when the state, which has the responsiblity for the road as far as Hāna Town, began repaving and improving it.

The curves stayed the same. The one-lane bridges were left alone. While Hāna Highway was made passable and reasonably safe, it is still adventure enough to limit the flow of traffic.

"Last Chance" for gas, Pāʻia, by local artist Wendy Brody.

Modern-day Pā'ia town.

CHAPTER IV

ON A 'HIGHWAY TO HEAVEN'
FERN VALLEYS, WATERFALLS AND BAMBOO

There is no particular reason, historically or
geographically, to begin a tour of the Hāna Coast with
Pā'ia, except that nearly everyone does.

The road between Pā'ia and Hāna Town has been traveled by every conceivable vehicle: four-wheeled, two-wheeled, four-legged and on foot. Once a year, scores of runners get together for the Hāna Relays, a 55-mile foot race with teams of runners changing off during the run, which begins near the Ka-hului Airport and ends at Hāna Harbor. The rest of the year hikers hitch it and hoof it—more of the former than the latter although overt hitchhiking is illegal on Maui.

They all begin at Pā'ia, a ghost town that has refused to die. The name itself means "Noisy." During the 1930s Pā'ia was *the* town on Maui. It had a population of nearly 10,000 residents, most living in ethnic enclaves called "camps" that were strung up Baldwin Avenue toward Maka-wao. The camps were settlements of immigrant workers, mostly segregated by their countries of origin, with much of the camp housing built in 1910 for the arrival of the first Portuguese families.

Also up Baldwin Avenue, a railroad station survives, the building now supporting other uses. Sugar king Claus Spreckles built the Kahului Railroad Co. between 1881 and 1886, linking lower Pā'ia to Kahului Harbor and thus ending the need to ship sugar from Kū'au landing, just east of Pā'ia on the coast. Alexander & Baldwin, which took over Spreckles Hawaiian Commercial Co. in 1899, also took over the railroad and, in 1913, extended it past Ha'i-kū.

Until 1966, the railroad was used to haul cane into the mills at Pā'ia and molasses to the harbor. It was also used for passengers, taking school children from Ha'i-kū to the big Maui High School located in Hāmākua Poko and St. Anthony's School in Wai-luku.

The dwindling of the robust, often rowdy plantation town into the quiet, crossroads neighborhood of today began with the opening of Frank Baldwin's "Dream City" in Ka-hului. The first-time availability of residential lots prompted many Pā'ia residents to abandon the plantation-supplied camp housing.

As soon as possible, the camp housing was demolished, and sugar cane fields were planted where homes once stood.

While the fields nibbled away at the outskirts, the commercial center of the town persisted. Today on the Hāna Highway "mainstreet" is a series of last-chance gas stations and restaurants, interspersed with the sort of clever, colorful art specialty shops that come and go with the regularity of the tide. The old Paia Mercantile Co., once the town's answer to a department store, has been converted into a graphic arts center and restaurant.

Pā'ia is the location of the last restaurants to be found on the highway to Hāna and a good place to stop for breakfast on a drive that began early in Ka-hului, Wai-luku or points farther west. It is a drive that must be begun early to be enjoyed, particularly if the other half of it, the drive out, is to be accomplished on the same day.

Down the highway a few minutes from Pā'ia is Kū'au, "Handle," which is the name of a point, a bay and a small residential community. The area has some tidal pools which, when the ocean is calm, are one of the few places along this coast of strong currents where children can safely swim. Old-time fishermen used to park their families by the pools while they went diving in the offshore reefs.

The primary attraction of Kū'au is the surf, and that is somewhat eclipsed by a spot a little farther down the road. Ho'okipa State Park is the recognized home of organized surfing on Maui and boasts some of the best winter surf on the island. The name Ho'okipa means "Hospitality," which the ocean there alternately offers and denies the surfers who line the bluffs to watch waves roll in. It's a place where "ding strings," the leashes that keep surfer and surfboard together in a kickout or a wipeout, are an absolute necessity.

Recently there was a chicken-skin incident involving an informal grave at Ho'okipa that actually could have happened almost anyplace along the Hāna Coast.

During the course of building some stone walls in the park, construction workers found human bones in the sand. This is not unusual on Maui. While ali'i were carefully buried by the ancients in hidden caves, common people were often buried anywhere and without markings. That day one of the workmen picked up what looked like a thigh bone and, before anyone could stop him, heaved it into the ocean.

As the crew was leaving the work site in the afternoon, that particular workman fell off a truck and broke his back, and not long after that lost his son at sea.

The typically Hawaiian explanation is that the man's problems were caused by unpropitiated spirits, and the accepted method of dealing with buried bones is to stop work and immediately call a clergyman. The particular faith is not as important as the clergyman's willingness to try and placate the spirit of the dead person. At various times recently, these rites have

Hoʻokipa—she of strong winds and wave conditions—is well
known internationally for her surfing and windsurfing conditions.

been performed by Shinto, Buddhist, Congregationalist, Roman Catholic, Methodist, Baptist, what-have-you, clergy.

In all instances, the bones are taken reverently from the site, with the clergyman interceding with the ʻaumakua, the spirits, and then they are reburied in an appropriate place nearby. As extreme as this may seem, it is the prudent thing to do.

There is no one, regardless of background or belief, who has lived many years on Maui without developing a healthy respect for the old places, the old ways and their disconcerting ability to intrude on modern times. Through the work of both nature and man, many *wahi pana*, sacred sites, are now changed beyond recognition. It is possible for someone to stand in the

Digging the Ditch

It takes a ton of water to produce one pound of sugar. To realize the promise of enormous landholdings in the arid central isthmus of Maui, Alexander & Baldwin needed water—lots of water.

The Sugar Reciprocity Treaty of 1876 made Hawai'i sugar production more lucrative and, thus, the construction of a massive irrigation system on Maui became financially feasible. That same year Alexander & Baldwin negotiated a lease with King Ka-lā-kaua to build an $80,000, 17-mile aqueduct across crown lands, from the watershed at Honopou and Nā'ili'ilihā'ele streams to dry Central Maui.

There was a gambler's catch in the lease: A & B had less than two years to get the job done or they would lose what they had built to the government, which, most likely, would turn it over to A & B's chief competitor, Claus Spreckles.

It was an imposing task. A crew of 200 men began almost immediately after the contract was signed.

Most of the construction was supervised by Henry P. Baldwin, even though during the project's planning stages he lost his right arm above the elbow in a mill accident. Various historians quote Baldwin cursing the machine and vowing, "You have handicapped me for life. Now I am going to make you support me."

The first job was to build a road to bring in the supplies necessary to construct an irrigation canal slashed across the face of a mountain and through tunnels carved out of live rock. Various sections of the ditch were linked by 24-inch pipes, waterproofed with blackpitch. Other sections, crossing some of the many gulches, were linked aerially by trestles.

The construction went smoothly until the crew reached Māliko Gulch, which was stretched across the very center of their path. There are several accounts describing that dramatic moment when Baldwin and his men first encountered the gulch.

The men were gathered on the Kai-lua side, looking down a 50-degree slope for 700 feet and then down the sides of the gulch yet another 250 feet.

These were not timid men. They had hacked their way through tunnels barely big enough to crawl through. They had felled great trees. They had built trestles above gulches filled with bone-breaking boulders. But now they saw that Baldwin expected water to flow uphill.

Baldwin explained the siphon action that would make it work, and as the men pondered this, they continued to eye the sometimes cloudy precipice that was to be their own perch for this chapter of the work.

Construction had to continue on schedule—even a few days' delay could cost Baldwin his entire project. The men stood fast, and Baldwin took the only recourse left to a leader without followers. He scrambled over the lip of the gulch himself, clutching the heavy rope with his good left hand and cross-gripping the rope with his ankles.

First one man and then another, watching the crippled *haole* work his way down the rope, took hold with his own two hands and followed.

In the days after, as sections of pipe were handed down the slope and up the other side by men dangling from ropes, Baldwin made it a point to go down the rope at least once a day.

The project was completed on time, winding across Hāmākua Poko, across Ha'i-kū, below Hāli'i-maile and up and across the area that lies just below present-day Puka-lani. Sixty-million gallons of water a day came through the ditches, making a fortune for A & B, whose firm remains the largest private land owner on the island of Maui.

The coastline near Pāʻia, looking toward West Maui.

midst of a *wahi pana* and not know it, and anyone exploring beyond the shoulders of the road should do so with more than just simple caution . . . should do so with respect and *aloha* for the spirits who may be guarding the land.

Just past Hoʻokipa, Hāna Highway swoops to the right and down into Māliko Gulch, home of a famous historical event. The gulch runs from high on the mountain down to the bay, where every year during the Queen Kaʻahu-manu Festival teams of women canoe paddlers set off on an "iron woman" race to Ka-hului Harbor.

This great crease in the side of the mountain became the last major obstacle in the path of Henry P. Baldwin and Samuel Alexander in their ambitious sugar enterprise in the late 19th Century.

The Hāna Highway climbs out of Māliko Gulch on an asphalt ramp, cuts through the side of the gulch under a stand of ironwood trees and out into an expanse of pineapple fields that typify the Haʻi-kū area, home of

the last of the independent pineapple growers and the first of the small-plot diversified farmers.

Out on the bluffs at the sea end of the pineapple fields is a Coast Guard light. Once it was a lighthouse, but now it is one of those automatic affairs that operates without benefit of human attention.

Off to the left is Paʻu-wela Point, the west side of a small bay. The point is one of several spots in East Maui where ghosts described as marching warriors are said to appear. On certain nights these apparitions are said to arise on the east side of the promontory and march across the point of land to the west, where they are said to disappear.

The Haʻi-kū Community Center is just across the highway from the pineapple road that borders the top of a gulch leading down to Kuiʻaha Bay, a traditional fishing spot in the area.

For years local residents used a trail that wound down through the pastureland to

A family picnic, Wai-lua.

the bay, allowing them to hike down to the rocky beach and spend the day fishing and skin diving for lobster. The trail cuts through land that was ultimately leased to a wealthy doctor who put a gate across it, complaining that people on the trail had bothered his livestock. A group of Hawaiians protested the ban, and eventually the county agreed to intercede and either obtain the leaseholders' permission to use the trail or else to secure right-of-access in the courts. More than a half-dozen years later, the issue is still unresolved.

The scattering of buildings along the highway is called Pa'u-wela or lower Ha'i-kū. Ha'i-kū proper is some miles up Kokomo Road, past "Giggle Hill," an ancient cinder cone covered with pine trees. It got its name during World War II, when it was known as a trysting spot for the 4th Division Marines stationed at Camp Maui and their local girlfriends.

Ha'i-kū, which means "Speak Abruptly" or "Sharp Break," is at the edge of the Hāna Coast's rainy section, which begins here and runs all the way to Kī-pahulu. During times of adequate rain, it is an area of many small waterfalls and freshwater pools that are excellent for swimming and diving.

In ancient times it was a place of *koa* forests, a prime spot for canoe builders and feather gatherers looking for the *'ōhi'a-le-hua* and *'ōhi'a-'ai* trees that were home for the *'ō'ō* and *'amakihi* and the *'i'iwi*, endemic island birds prized by Hawaiian artisans for their feathers.

Now it is one of Maui's exurbias, an area of homes built during the 1970s on two-and-a-half-acre lots known legally as "agricultural subdivisions." The largest parcels of land belong to the state, a legacy of crown lands established during the monarchy. These lands are leased on the basis of competitive bids for pasturage and for the growing of pineapple.

At Kaupakulua Road, the real Hāna Highway of fable and song begins; 617 curves and 56 bridges east lies Hāna Town.

Actually, there are two experiences on the Hāna Highway.

One is reserved for the driver, who must stay alert for oncoming vehicles behind blind curves, where the road is one-and-a-half vehicles wide. The rule, when meeting an oncoming vehicle is to edge yours as far to the right as you can and still keep on moving and to hope that the other driver does the same.

For a driver, the Hāna Highway is a twist of asphalt, spun along a background of side-sweeping masses of green-on-green foliage, interspersed with swatches of blue from the sea or sky.

For a passenger, particularly one traveling in an open vehicle, the Hāna Highway experience is a physical assault on all five senses. Inches away from your swaying vehicle are masses of rain forest plants— ginger, *liliko'i*, guava, *'ōhi'a-'ai* (mountain apple) and others—sending off clouds of pungent aromas.

The road doesn't so much cross the land as it burrows—through a tunnel of green.

Several miles of twists and turns later, a school bus shelter in a right-hand curve marks the old Hawaiian community of Huelo, site of the Haka-kau-pueo Congregational Church. The church's name, which means "Resting Perch of an Owl," is a reference to the diurnal Hawaiian owls which habitually perch in a nearby *hala* grove.

From Huelo, the highway winds two miles to Kai-lua, the headquarters for the East Maui Irrigation Co. and a literal mecca for wild pig hunters.

At Kau-mahina State Park, about eight miles down the highway, the road suddenly climbs into the sky. At the right-hand turn, just past the park with its paper-bark trees, there is a remarkable view across Hono-manū Bay to the west side of the Ke-'anae Peninsula.

A Heliconia, or "lobster claw," found near Wai-lua.

From this point on into Hāna Town and beyond, the coast has been continuously inhabited from the earliest days of the Polynesian settlers.

Ke-'anae Valley stretches all the way up the mountain and into the crater on the top of Hale-a-ka-lā. Ke-'anae is usually translated "The Mullet," but Maui historian Inez Ashdown has another interpretation; she says it means "The Inheritance from Heaven," and she recounts an ancient story to explain the name.

According to Hawaiian legend, in the days when the gods first walked the islands, there was no water. In her book *Where I Live There Are Rainbows,* Ms. Ashdown tells a story in which Kāne, the creator, visits this particular area, thrusts his staff into solid rock and draws forth water.

In fact, it was the abundance of fresh water flowing down from the watersheds above that has made Ke-'anae a successful community. It is the site of many legendary exploits.

Taro fields quilt the Ke-'anae Peninsula.

One legend speaks of the existence of a powerful shark in Ke-'anae. The shark was often a symbol of power in ancient Hawai'i, worshipped as an 'aumakua, or protective spirit.

According to this story, two families in the area used to exchange food, a common practice, the couple living seaside at Ke-'anae giving fish and the couple living upland giving garden produce.

One day the woman from the shore gave her sister-in-law on the hillside nothing but a fishtail in exchange for bananas and sweet potatoes. The woman took the fishtail home in her calabash, saying nothing about the scanty trade.

That night both she and her husband dreamed of a shark, and when they woke up in the morning they found a live shark swimming around in the calabash, where only a tail had been the night before.

The excited couple freed the shark in an upland pool and made offerings to it. During a heavy rain, the shark was washed *down to the ocean, where, according to legend, it lives to this day in an underground cave near the Ke-'anae wharf.*

Since the beginning, the rains that fall into the Ke-'anae Valley have fed the peninsula and the people who worked the land.

In ancient times, the Ke-'anae Peninsula was a place of many fishponds. Above the peninsula and back into the valley, Hawaiians terraced the land and grew taro and bananas and yams.

The life blood of the successful crops was the water flowing fresh and pure to the ocean and the sweat of the men and women who dug, cultivated and harvested.

The peninsula began taking on its modern day appearance around the turn of the century when the Chinese men who came to work on the sugar plantations satisfied their contracts and went out on their own. They turned the ponds into rice paddies. They married local women and began

"Summer Fun" participants at Ke-ʻanae Elementary School.

many of the families that call Ke-ʻanae/ Wai-lua home today.

Still later, the rice paddies were turned into taro fields, still relying on the carefully channeled and diverted stream waters to feed the aquatic plants.

At various times, watercress farming has also been carried out in the Ke-ʻanae area, which is most notable in recent times as a redoubt of Hawaiian culture and folkways.

Ke-ʻanae school, one of the smallest in the entire state, was one of the first to have a resident *kūpuna*. In the early 1970s, fully 10 years before such programs were instituted in other schools, Ke-ʻanae school children were learning the chants and folkways of their ancestors.

The traditions of a Hawaiian past are strong in the Ke-ʻanae area where nearly everyone is related to someone else. It is a place of family efforts.

Until the late 1970s, taro was a marginal business due to low prices. Then, with the rise in ethnic identity among Hawaiians,

taro and *poi* began to sell again. A new *poi* factory opened up on the Big Island started offering higher prices to farmers, making taro a going, growing enterprise.

In 1981, the taro farmers at Ke-ʻanae were threatened with a loss of their water. The streams and channels feeding into the taro patches had become clogged with *hau* and weeds. A call to the community turned out scores of machete and chain-saw wielding volunteers to clean out the stream beds.

Even with the higher prices paid for taro, keeping a family fed, clothed and educated requires the efforts of all the family. Most often, the men work for the county or the state highway departments. Their wives take care of the house and work in the fields until the men can get home. Families raise a few head of beef for the table. Some women pick *ʻopihi* to sell and to make jewelry from the shells. Some men maintain their families by driving daily down the Hāna Highway to jobs as far away as Kāʻana-pali, the point farthest west on

Harry Mitchell.

A Son of Ke-'anae

Harry Mitchell was born in Ke-'anae in 1919, was raised as the *hānai*, adopted, son of a neighboring family and lives in the area to this day, pulling about six bags of taro a week from his two-acre *kuleana*. He greets two *haole* strangers with an *aloha* that is specifically Hawaiian, slicing and stir-frying fresh taro chips and putting on more water for coffee because what is left in the thermos from morning isn't hot enough for hospitality. His jeans hanging slackly over his *'ōkole,* he alternately turns the taro chips and sets out cheese, condensed milk, sugar, and saloon pilot crackers—island staples, stored in giant mayonnaise jars, excellent cannisters in an area known for its wetness.

Like his Hawaiian ancestors before him, Mitchell knows how to live on the Hāna Coast. He recognizes the value of his understanding, and as he shares his food he is lamenting the passage of the intelligence that is Hawaiian.

"There are very few left who know how to read the moon and the stars now," he says. "The old Hawaiians took what they knew from nature ... I think even our women learned to dance the *hula* by watching palm trees in the wind . . . Our ancestors would rest seven days each month by the moon; and they would rest the land, too. But there aren't many people left who can teach these things."

Harry Mitchell is quite active in Hawaiian and community affairs, as are many young Hawaiians now developing a deep interest in learning and living the old ways. He is respected for his knowledge and also for his songs, composed on a guitar in celebration of his beloved Hawai'i. One of his favorites is *Nā Ko'olau,* a six-stanza gem that leaps across the entire Hāna Coast, one verse at a time. Mitchell wrote out the song and his translation for his visitors that morning.

Nā Ko'olau

'I ke 'ia ika nani o na pali uliuli
(I see my beautiful green mountain)
Aloha ku'u home o na Ko'olau
(I love my mountain home
in Ko'olau)
E huli māua i Wai-'ānapanapa
(Then two of us travel to
Wai-'ānapanapa)
He wai lūkini 'ānapanapa mai nei
(The fragrant glistening waters
ripple in the wind)
Kū mai ka pu'u o Ka-'uiki
(Ka-'uiki hill stands upright)
'O Hāna 'iu'iu pōhai ke aloha
(And Hāna lives in peace with my
love)
Kau mai ke ānuenue i Kau-pō
(I see a rainbow over Kau-pō)
Pā mai ka makani kā'ili aloha
(The gentle wind caresses me and I
take the feeling of love)

Sharks caught off the Hāna Coast.

Maui, making them eligible for the dubious distinction of being the longest-haul commuters in the islands.

The Chinese legacy on the Hāna Coast lives on with many Chinese surnames carried by Hawaiian families and many apparently Hawaiian surnames actually being Hawaiianized Chinese.

It is not uncommon on the Hāna Coast for one brother to spell his name in the Hawaiian fashion (for instance, Apuna) while another brother spells it in the Chinese fashion (Ah Puna).

One of the oldest churches on Maui is the stone Congregationalist Church on the Ke-'anae Peninsula. It was built in 1856 as a part of a circuit ministered by preachers who traveled from community to community and restored recently by members of Ke-'anae's Pahukoa family.

A little farther down the road is St. Gabriel's at Wai-lua, one of the first stops for Roman Catholic priests in the islands.

Wai-lua, which means "Two Waters," is actually the name of two places on the Hāna Coast. The Wai-lua near Ke-'anae is comprised of Wai-lua Iki and Wai-lua Nui—that is, "Small" Wai-lua and "Big" Wai-lua. (The other Wai-lua is located in Kī-pahulu, on the other side of Hāna Town.) This particular area is known as the home of a legendary demon of Hawai'i, a "shark-man."

The ancient Hawaiians believed that a shark-man could change himself from man to shark and back again. He was thought to live in communities unnoticed, warning swimmers against sharks and, if his warnings went unheeded, himself becoming a man-eating monster. The only sign that differentiated a shark-man from an ordinary person is a shark's mouth, which he bore on his back—usually kept covered by a kapa.

One of the many ancient stories of shark-men is the tale of Pau-walu, who is said to have lived at Wai-lua. True to his

name, which meant "Eight Dead," Pau-walu would warn fishermen going to sea that eight of them were about to die. Each time his prophecy came true.

The people of the village suspected Pau-walu, but none would confront him until Akeake, one of Maui's earliest heroes, heard about the suspicious deaths. Akeake was a small man, and when he challenged Pau-walu the demon laughed at him. But Akeake was powerful, and he ripped the kapa *from Pau-walu's body, exposing the shark's mouth on his back, threw him into a fire and destroyed him.*

Since the completion of the highway along this side of the Hāna Coast, a traditional stop off point is Pua'a-ka'a ("Rolling Pig") State Park. Before the highway was paved with asphalt, *haole* drivers who had forced their vehicles along the twisting track bastardized the name of the park into "Poor Car."

On the other side of Pua'a-ka'a State Park lies the village of Nā-hiku. It's a collection of scattered homes today, but at the beginning of this century it was a thriving plantation town, growing not sugar, but rubber.

In 1899, the Nahiku Rubber Co. began planting thousands of experimental rubber trees on the *makai* side of the highway, and after tests indicated the probability of being able to produce money-making rubber, the Nahiku Co. was incorporated in 1905.

The American and Koolau rubber companies were also established on a smaller scale in the area, and at one time there were more than 25,000 rubber trees of several varieties growing in and around Nā-hiku. A lot of them remain to this day although they are now shrouded by later growths of guava and *hau.* At the height of its tenure as the first and only rubber plantation town in the United States, Nā-hiku boasted a Chinese grocery-post office, a plantation general store, individual churches for Protestant, Roman Catholic

and Mormon worshippers and a school-house with an enrollment of 20.

There were also assorted workers' and plantation managers' homes and a rubber processing shed where the raw latex was cleaned and steamed and formed into slabs for the mule-drawn wagon trip to Hāna and shipment out.

The venture was of great interest, not only in Hawai'i, but in Washington, D.C., where Department of Agriculture officials did what they could to assist.

The rubber companies began winding down in 1912, citing high labor costs as a reason. One of their former field workers, John Kaiwi, recalls that a 10-hour day with a 30-minute lunch break netted him only 50 cents. He said that the real reason for rubber's failure on the Hāna Coast was the rain—"Too wet," he said, "The rubber was no good."

Kaiwi said that after the rubber was *pau,* finished, the residents planted cash crop bananas; then after the bananas they planted roselle for jelly. When the roselle didn't work, people in Nā-hiku started to move away.

Among some circles on Maui, Nā-hiku is now known for a crop of a different sort—*Cannabis sativa,* known locally as *pakalōlō,* which means "crazy tobacco." It is customary for the Maui Police Department to go over the area thoroughly each year during its "Green Harvest" marijuana eradication program. Using National Guard helicopters, the police first survey the place from the air and then drop down to pick the illegal crops.

Just on the other side of Nā-hiku, the land turns into the kind of topography most often associated with Hāna—rolling slopes pressing up against the mountain and sliding easily down to the sea. Along the coast, remnants of ancient Hawaiian foot highways can still be traversed by hikers.

The lands of the area, flattened and smoothed by early Hawaiians and later sugar and pineapple farmers, make admirable pastures and locations for facilities such as the airport and the new Hāna Elementary and High School.

The airport provides an easy way in for some visitors to the Hāna Coast and there are a few well-heeled residents who commute to work outside via air. During 1985, 20,971 passengers went through the small facility.

From Nā-hiku to Kau-pō, there are numerous *heiau* sites. They are particularly thickly set in the area right around Hāna Town since it was customary for chiefs going into battle to build a *heiau* as a dedication to the gods and, if successful, to build another in gratitude.

Depending on who is doing the counting and what criteria are used, there are some 25 historically significant Hawaiian sites in the four-mile stretch from the Hāna Airport to the village of Hāmoa.

As mentioned earlier, the largest *heiau* in the state is located at Honomanū in the area of coast on the Ke'anae side of the airport. Called the Pi'i-lani-hale Heiau, it consists of a stone platform 340 feet by 415 feet, terraced in a fashion unseen elsewhere. The highest, north, side of the *heiau* is some 50 feet from the bottom of the hill. The south and west sides were enclosed by a wall 10 feet high and 8 to 10 feet thick. The top was paved with small pebbles and chunks of lava. At the northwest corner, a paved footpath led up the slope to the *heiau*, which dates from around the 15th Century.

Nearby Wai-'ānapanapa State Park is a beautiful and popular cabin and tent camping spot for Mauians who want to get away for a time of walking old trails, staring at the sea and exploring water-filled caves.

Wai-'ānapanapa, the name of the coastal state park, a famous cave within it and also a series of small lakes 6,800 feet up near the top of Hale-a-ka-lā in the Hāna Forest Preserve, means "Glistening Water."

The kūpuna tell of a time when Ka'akea, a chief notorious for his cruelty, was jealous of the affection his wife, Pōpō-'alaea, had for her younger brother. There was much gossip, and the chief threatened to kill his wife.

Pōpō-'alaea tried to escape by hiding in one of the caves at Wai-'ānapanapa, but one of her attendants made a fatal mistake. In an effort to distract her distraught mistress, the attendant was waving a kāhili, a feather-topped standard used to fan royalty in Hawai'i. She moved the royal symbol a little too far toward the entrance of the cave, and a calm pool outside reflected the brightly colored feathers.

Ka'akea saw the reflection, recognized the distinctive form and realized that it had to be his wife inside. He killed her in a bloody, brutal fashion.

It is said that on the night of Kū, the Hawaiian god of justice, the water in the pool runs red. And in the spring, the time of year when the murder took place, a gathering of

Posing for pictures, Wai-'ānapanapa State Park.

red shrimp causes the stones to turn red, a sign to the Hawaiians of forgiveness or the casting out of an evil spirit.

Three-quarters of a mile north of Wai-'ānapanapa Cave, near the shore and on the old Kiha-a-pi'ilani foot highway, is the Kau-ke-ali'i Heiau, a large open platform about four feet high.

A little farther east lies a *heiau* where it is said that the sound of drums can be heard on certain nights.

The most important spot on this section of the Hāna Coast for a Hawaiian in trouble with the ruling chiefs or, perhaps, a priest, was the area near where Ka'ahu-manu spent her childhood two centuries ago and where the Hāna Medical Center is located today. This is the place of the Kāni'o-moku Heiau, a *pu'uhonua*, a place of refuge.

At Ka'ina-limu, on the rocky point north of Hāna Bay, there is an unusual double *heiau*, identified as Kau-lei-lepo/Kau-lei-'ula.

It consisted of two elevated platforms connected by a 25-foot long causeway. The larger platform is 42 by 54 feet, about twice the size of the smaller platform, and is terraced at one point to a height of 15 feet.

Situated along the highway between Wai-'ānapanapa and Hāna Town are also several of Hāna's modern-day enterprises, including Helani Gardens, which is not only a large commercial nursery but also a garden open for public tours. A sign at the entrance says, "Don't hurry. Don't worry. And don't forget to smell the flowers." The gardens are owned and operated by Howard F. Cooper as a legacy from his father, the Cooper mentioned earlier as a mayor of Hāna Town. The elder Cooper was murdered on his way to work one morning in 1916, long before he could realize his dream of planting a large land tract with papaya, bananas, avocado and citrus. The current garden, filled as it is with flowering shrubs and fish ponds and bridges and trees—lots of trees—is a fitting memorial.

The terraced walls of Pi'i-lani-hale Heiau, the largest ancient place
of Hawaiian worship in Hawaii, are still intact.

"Hana Store," a painting by Robert Eskridge, on
display in the lobby of the Hotel Hana-Maui.

A country roadway through Hāna's lush Helani Gardens.

CHAPTER V

LIFE AND LOVE IN HĀNA TOWN
'NEATH LOW-LYING SKIES AND A GUARDIAN HILL

Just before Hāna Town, the highway divides. A
white on green sign, the stencil work of a county
employee, helpfully informs the driver that either
road will lead into the heart of Hāna.

Both roads pass the county government's main physical presence in the *moku*, a combination police station/highway department and court house/administrative facility Just beyond it to the right lies an informal graveyard of county vehicles worn to rust in unceasing labor on the roads. The road then opens into the pasture which lines the *mauka* side of Hāna Town.

To the left, the road passes the old courthouse and jail, both currently undergoing restoration. Local residents have always said they knew when the jail held a prisoner because then the surrounding yard was particularly neat. Adjacent to these two structures is a modest facility housing the Hāna Cultural Center. Founded in 1971 by Mrs. John Hanchett, known to her friends as "Babes", this historic preservation group now boasts more than 300 members and is actively involved in collecting and displaying photographs, texts, implements and other objects and artifacts of old Hāna.

Then the road dips down toward the bay, the true heart of Hāna.

The right side of Hāna Bay is formed by the fortress-hill Ka-'uiki, one of the most visible remnants of the Hāna Volcanic Series, a late cinder cone on the east rift zone of Hale-a-ka-lā.

The sea, with its tireless determination, has worn away a large portion of the old cone, exposing its iron-rich red lava interior. The hill was covered with bunch grass in ancient times, making it a bit more accessible than it is today with its cloak of ironwood trees.

In the time when wars were fought hand-to-hand, Ka-'uiki was a natural stronghold that figured heavily in the many-battled history of Hāna.

"This hill is famous," wrote historian Abraham Fornander in his work *The Polynesian Race,* "for it is a natural fort and people on it are generally safe from assault, being protected on all sides by steep and inaccessible cliffs."

In the 18th Century, when the Big Island's Ka-lani-'ōpu'u held Hāna, Ka-heki-li's forces fought their way to the foot of Ka-'uiki and were initially stymied.

Direct assault, difficult in and of itself, was further complicated by a ruse by which Ka-lani-'ōpu'u capitalized on the deep Hawaiian regard for the spirit world. He had a large wooden figure with a fiercesome countenance erected each night to defend the hill.

The trick worked until one of Ka-hekili's men gathered his courage and crept up on the huge figure. The warrior named Pi'imaiwa'a began to rap the head of this image with the tip of his club, and, when he heard the sound of wood striking wood, he realized it was a trick.

He began to hit the statue with force, calling out, "Death by Pi'imaiwa'a." The image fell to the sands below, and to this day the spot *mauka* of Ka-'uiki is called Kāwala-ki'i, "Toppling Image."

This is the battle Ka-hekili won by cutting off Ka-lani-'ōpu'u's supply of water.

Ka-hekili had control of Hāna for only a few years before Maui's first recorded contact with western man. Capt. James Cook had visited other islands in early 1778 before sailing north to find a passage across the North American continent.

When Cook's ships, the HMS *Resolution* and HMS *Discovery* returned to the islands in November of that year, news of the astounding "sailing islands" had circulated to the far corners of the Hawaiian chain. On his return trip, Cook's ships cruised for two months along the coasts of the Big Island and Maui.

It was common, in those days, to have a lookout posted on Ka-'uiki and, in light of the on-going struggles between Ka-hekili and Ka-lani-'ōpu'u, it is likely that a Hawaiian sentinel first spotted the returning ships from atop Ka-'uiki.

It is recorded that fleets of canoes were paddled out from Hāna to the ships. It was directly off Ka-'uiki that Ka-mehameha boarded Cook's ship. Some say it was Ka-mehameha who directed Cook to his destiny at Ke-ala-ke-kua on the Big Island.

As history surged around Ka-'uiki, the hill played an important, if more mundane, role in the day-to-day life of Hawaiians.

Until relatively recent times, a *kilo i'a,* fish spotter, would be posted on Ka-'uiki to watch for the schools of *akule,* mullet, that swam into the harbor.

Using hand signals or white flags and shouting, the *kilo i'a* would alert the village when the *akule* were running. The whole town would turn out for the *hukilau,*

an event that took place almost weekly and, many times, supplied all of the protein needed to augment the foods that were grown on land.

At a call from the spotter, fishing canoes drawn up on the beach were put into the water. Over the years the dugout canoes that were once used by Hawaiians have given way to vessels with square hulls built from milled lumber.

The canoes would take the nets out and around the school of fish, following the directions of the spotter up on Ka-'uiki. Once the fish were encircled, the nets were drawn to shore, where the water was shallow enough to stand. Everyone took a hand in drawing them onto the beach and retrieving the bounty.

Everyone worked, although it was more like play, and everyone got a share — even those too old or infirm to leave home. Runners would deliver the fish, gills still moving, to the *kūpuna.*

In former years, as now, the bay was a recreation site. William Haia Chang, a columnist for the *Maui News,* reminisced about the bay in the years immediately following World War II:

> Every Fourth of July, there was a celebration at the bay. We had canoe races, "tin-boat" races and swimming races as well as "tug-o-war" contests on the sand ...
>
> The "tin boats" were constructed from corrugated iron roofing sheets hammered flat. These were shaped into boats by nailing the metal to pieces of wood at the bow and stern and sealing the holes with tar collected from the road edges. Usually these boats were propelled with two-hand paddles made of flat pieces of wood. Roof shingles were a favorite because they were light. Most of the boats were very simply made to hold

Ka-'uiki Hill and, beyond, Hāna Bay.

one individual, but some were quite elaborate and large enough to hold two and three, sometimes with outriggers and painted with an array of designs and colors.

The arrival of the aluminum roof spelled the end to the tin boats. The aluminum, while serving better as roofing material, was too flexible for use as a boat hull.

The bay is now populated by surfers and teams of canoe racers—some of the best in the state—plying the waters with 40-foot fiberglass racing canoes.

The *hukilau* has been replaced by a handful of men using Citizen Band radio links with a spotter and small boats. A boat is used to drop the net around the *akule*. Another boat is used to frighten the fish into the net, where they are caught in the squares of nylon cord and hauled aboard.

Fishing is still as much a sport as an industry for the people of the Hāna Coast, with handfuls of men regularly going to sea in small boats to harvest the sea's crops. It is not a pastime to be taken lightly.

In February, 1979, five Hāna Coast residents, in the prime of life, loaded their gear into the 16-foot Boston Whaler Sarah Joe, *and took off to do some trolling. That afternoon a storm blew in: 40 knot winds that whipped the channel to waves so deep that John Hanchett, father of one of the crewmen and organizer of the first search party, said, "It was the worst ocean I've ever been in. We could have been 50 yards from them out there, and we wouldn't have been able to see them."*

The Coast Guard came in about 5 p.m. with a helicopter and C-130 search plane and scoured the sea, continuing daily for a week. When the Coast Guard gave up, Hāna Coast residents launched their own search, which they continued for another week until they, too—in anguish—finally gave up. The Sarah Joe *and her crew disappeared without a trace.*

Ka-'uiki: A Love Story

The first time Māui visited Hāna, it is said that he fell in love with the beauty of the *'āina* and resolved to spend the rest of his days in this graceful land.

One morning after Māui and his wife had settled on the low hill in back of Hāna, the great magician sat marveling at the beauty below. He was struck by the sight of a gentle gray mist sweeping over the bay. The sunlight struck the raindrops and shattered into a mass of brilliant colors so beautiful that when his daughter was born a few days later, Māui named her Noenoe Ua Kea O Hāna, "Misty, Light Rains of Hāna."

Time passed, and Noenoe grew rapidly into a beauty. She loved the sea, and spent much time there.

Near the beach that Noenoe visited there was a pool of blue and silver sweet water. As she passed, the eyes of a handsome youth were filled with her loveliness, but none dared the wrath of Māui by approaching his daughter and so the youth kept his presence a secret from the maiden.

It was an easy secret to keep—Noenoe averted her eyes when passing the pool, as she had been warned that the place was inhabited by *Menehune,* a mythical tribe of mischievous elves.

One day Noenoe stayed longer than usual at the beach, and the moon had started its climb into the sky before she began to walk home. As she passed the pool, she was halted by the sounds of laughter.

Hiding behind a large rock, she cautiously peered at the pool in the silvery gleam of the full moon and saw what no human eye had ever beheld: hundreds of *Menehune* dancing and frolicking in the pool. As she watched, a shadow passed her eye and she looked up into the face of the handsome youth. She started to run away.

"Wait, Noenoe," he said. "You have broken the law of the *Menehune,* and you shall not escape them. Come with me, and I will help you."

In the cool glow of the moon, Noenoe saw the love in his eyes, and, although she had never seen him before, she knew he was Ka-'uiki, the *hānai* son of the *Menehune* who guarded him jealously. He had come to them on the waves and so they believed him to be a gift from Kanaloa, the sea god.

Noenoe fell in love with Ka-'uiki in that first magic instant. Ka-'uiki led Noenoe safely away from the *Menehune,* and the young lovers planned a life together.

Māui became aware of the romance and confronted his daughter. "This cannot be," he said. "Ka-'uiki is *kapu.* He is of the sea, and to the sea he must return some day."

The thought of being separated from Ka-'uiki filled Noenoe's eyes with pain, and Māui took pity on the lovers. He used his magic to keep them together forever.

He changed Ka-'uiki into a high hill, rooting him permanently in the *'āina* near the spot Māui himself so loved. His beloved daughter Māui changed into the misty, gentle rains that, to this day, cling to Ka-'uiki, caressing its high cliffs and slopes.

It is said the sea tells the story of Noenoe and Ka-'uiki when it sighs against the shore.

There is another, contradictory legend concerning Māui and the mountain Ka-'uiki, which is also a love story. It tells of the time when Māui stood on the mountain and, to impress a young woman, pushed up the heavens. As Martha Beckwith writes in her text *Hawaiian Mythology,* "The sky pressed down over the earth. A man 'supposed to be Maui' says to a woman that if she will give him a 'drink from her gourd' . . . he will push the sky up for her." The woman complies, and the man thrusts the sky upward. Thus, the legend concludes, though clouds may hang low over the mountain Hale-a-ka-lā, they never touch Ka-'uiki.

Legendary ʻĀ-lau Island.

One of the most famous exploits in the legendary history of the Hāna Coast took place off Hāmoa near 'Ā-lau Island.

Māui, a mythic figure common in all of Polynesian lore, was half-man, half-god. He was much loved by the fire goddess, Pele, and was known for his tricks and great feats of magic.

According to legend, the Hawaiian Islands were actually brought up from the bottom of the sea by Māui, with the help of a magic fishhook and his three brothers.

As it is told, Māui and his brothers paddled their canoe into the open ocean until they came to a certain spot. Māui baited his hook with an 'alae, the mudhen who brought fire to the people. Māui swung the magic hook with its sacred bait around and around in the air, finally letting it strike the ocean with a terrific splash.

The magic hook sank into the deep and became stuck in the bottom. Māui ordered his brothers: "Paddle as hard as you can, and don't look back!"

His brothers hauled in an enormous piece of land, emerging from the sea at the end of the line. One of the brothers was overcome with curiosity and looked back and at that the massive piece of land shattered into pieces—the islands.

Māui's magic fishhook, Mānai 'ikalani, which means "Made Fast to the Heavens," is still visible as a great group of stars lying along the path of the sun. Those ignorant of Māui's exploits think the stars make up the constellation Scorpius.

The demi-god Māui is also credited with the creation of Ka-'uiki, the guardian hill.

Hāna Bay at Ka-'uiki's base has been a popular surfing spot as long as there has been surfing. There is a peculiarity in the bay: the waves come in a certain distance and then stop.

According to local legend, there once was a chief from Tahiti who wanted to go surfing but found the water flat. He asked the gods to bring the waves, and when they did he began to surf.

On the shore were two young girls who, seeing the handsome chief, immediately fell in love with him. Vying with each other to display their charms, they removed their pā'ū. When the chief caught sight of the two naked girls, he was so startled that he stopped before reaching the shore, and the wave went no farther.

And to this day the surf of Hāna Bay does not go beyond that spot.

The gentle serenity of Hāna Bay has often been broken by human doings. There were battles fought, akule caught, and then there were the cattle drives.

With the demise of the sugar plantations at the end of World War II and the rise of the Hana Ranch, one of the most uproarious events in Hāna came when the pipi, cattle, were driven down to the bay to be loaded on ships.

The cattle were driven through Hāna Town with a paniolo stationed in each driveway to make sure the cows didn't trespass too badly.

The cowboys herded the cattle down the road into the bay and out onto the wharf, but sometimes the cattle had other ideas. They ran across the beach and into the water. The cowboys would follow them in and continue herding them in the water as they had on the land.

Water-borne cow punching was a technique commonly used up and down the Hāna Coast when the ships made stops in other places besides Hāna Bay. In places such as Nu'u, where there was no wharf, the cattle were driven into the ocean and then plucked out of the sea with slings and cranes to be loaded, bellowing their discontent, on board ships that would take them to markets in Honolulu.

Harry Hasegawa.

How You Figgah?

Nobody knows how Harry does it, but Harry does. He does it with a computer, and with Andy.

Harry, whose last name is Hasegawa, is the proprietor of an insanely cluttered general store in Hāna that has become quite famous and has even had a song written about it. No one has written a song about the computer, but Harry has written a speech about it, which he delivers to other business people who want to learn about such things. No one has written either a song or a speech about Andy, but they probably should.

A good place to start writing about Hasegawa General Store is by explaining that it is divided into two parts, unsurprisingly known as "the front" and "the back". "The front" is where you will find all of the stuff that inspired the song. There are rifles, soda-pop, pickled cabbage, *palaka* shirts, fishing poles, blanket bindings, screw-top wines, Band-Aids, batteries and baby bottles. I mean you

name it and Harry probably has it. Most of the people who shop in "the front" think that "the back" is just a warehouse, but this is also where the more utilitarian part of the store's merchandise is kept. Paint, nails, barbed wire, horse shoes, lumber, chain saws, wheelbarrows and parts by the thousands.

Harry sits up at the entrance to the store, which is also the exit. He mostly does paper work, answers the phone and listens to the cash registers chirp. There are two of the latter, monumentally-sized and umbilically connected to Harry's computer. Between them, they totally dominate the checkout counter, a subnominal affair which has been designed without any place to set anything down at all. Outgoing customers are thus forced to stand balancing armfuls of intended purchases while the registers chirp out an a cappella chorus of electric high-tech efficiency that is totally contradictory to the disquieting arrangement of the store itself. As might be ex-

"Andy" Olivera.

Going up the slope away from Hāna Bay, the old Hāna School lies to the left of the road leading up to the highway. The Hāna Community Association began working in the early 1980s to turn the historic school-house into a cultural center, which would serve as a place where the past could be remembered, the present served and the future planned. There were, however, some minor problems.

The project was complicated and slowed by the fact that the abandoned school was the property of the state, but with all of the documents finally in place, all of the structures were repaired and restored with county funds. The cultural center appears to be serving a great many needs.

Former classrooms have been turned over to the various clubs and organizations that colour Hāna's social fabric, and on a recent evening, activities at the complex included hula lessons, computer classes, a community association meeting and, in the kitchen of the old cafeteria, a group of Girl Scouts making guava jelly.

pected, uninitiated incoming customers are often in lost awe.

The computer absorbs all of the information that the cash registers fire into its bowels, then tells Harry what is in stock, what he needs to order, how much it costs, how much he needs to charge and how much profit he has made. But it doesn't tell him where anything is. That's where Andy comes in.

Andy is Hasegawa's head stock clerk and is usually in "the back". He has worked there for 25 years and is the only person in the store who knows where everything is. Not only that, he knows colors, models, serial numbers, lengths, widths, and weights.

Whenever a customer asks how to find a particular item, Harry reaches over, hits the switch of a vintage squawk box and yells, "**Andy!**" From somewhere in the back, Andy always yells, "**What?**"

Well, as they say, so much for electronics.

—Carl Lindquist

Up on the highway, the commercial center of Hāna is located along a stretch that is no more than three city blocks. The Hāna Ranch Center marks the right-hand end — as you are coming up from the bay — and it ends at the Hasegawa General Store.

The Hāna Sugar Mill was located just beyond Hasegawa's, *mauka* of the highway. Sparse remnants of the plantation complex remain, although nearly all traces of the old plantation camps have long since disappeared, marked here and there by an individual homesite.

On the south side of Hāna Town, State Road 36 becomes County Road 31 as it slides along the bottom of the foothills above Hāmoa, a which is a place that is also rich in native lore.

A left turnoff on the county highway leads down a narrow paved road to Hāmoa

Natural sea arch, Leho'ula.

Village and the beach where the Hotel Hāna-Maui maintains facilities for its guests. (Others who surf or swim there reach the spot from rocks at the end of the point.) The road runs along the base of Ka-iwi-o-Pele, the remnant of a cinder cone overlooking the field that was Hāna's first airport. Tucked into the side of the mount are two big microwave dish antennae, conversing with like facilities on the Big Island across 'Ale-nui-hāhā Channel. Through modern technology the ancient links forged between Hāna and the Big Island remain.

Ka-iwi-o-Pele, which means "The Bone of Pele" is said to be the site where the pig god Kama-pua'a ravished Pele; where, later, Pele fought with her older sister, Nā-maka-o-Kaha'i; and where the god Lono-muku climbed into the heavens to live on the moon.

This section of the coast is also known for the surf of Pu'u-hele, a name which means a "Traveling Hill".

Just offshore from Ka-iwi-o-Pele is 'Ā-lau Island, a four-acre landmark said to have been created by Pele when she broke open the side of the cinder cone which was named for her. 'Ā-lau is also thought to be a fragment of the land mass that shattered when the demi-god Māui "fished up" the islands.

This **area of** the Hāna Coast was home for two of the more important figures in Hawaiian history/legend, Kū-'ula and his son, Ai'ai.

Kū-'ula was considered a divine being in human form, and had a great *mana,* a divine power, over fish, the food of the sea. It is said that Kū-'ula devoted himself to fishing and invented the fishpond, so important to Hawaiian society. The ponds were shorelands encircled by rock walls and fed by waves—actually storage and breeding areas for mullet and other fish.

Kū-'ula's pond was built just south of Ka-iwi-o-Pele with a low rock wall about

Hotel Hana-Maui guest facilities, Hāmoa Beach.

300 yards long and arcing to a distance of 150 yards to sea. At high tide, the waves broke over the wall, which trapped the water, and what was in it, when the tide receded. A six-foot-wide gap in the seaward side could be closed with a net or matting. The walls of the pond were large enough and flat enough to accommodate small fishing shelters.

The ponds provided a ready source of protein and also provided the pond-tenders with something to exchange for the taro and sweet potatoes of inland farmers.

Kū-ʻulaʻs son, Aiʻai, came up with a technique that was also very important to Hawaiian fishermen but first he had to help his father rid the fishpond of a predator.

A large pūhi, *an eel, came to live in a sea cave near ʻAleamai and some distance out from the ʻĀ-lau rocks. The eel came to rob and destroy Kū-ʻulaʻs fishpond.*

Kū-ʻula decided to let his son, Aiʻai, handle the eel.

Aiʻai attached a hook to a long hau *rope and placed it at the entrance of the eelʻs cave. When the eel took the hook, Aiʻai signaled the people at Hane-oʻo and Hāmoa to pull their end of the rope and the people at ʻAleamai to pull their end.*

It is said that the ʻAleamai people won, landing the eel on the pāhoehoe *stones at Leho-ʻula. They endeavored to kill the prize without success; it took Aiʻai, who threw three* ʻalā *stones at the eel, to end its life.*

The eelʻs head was cut off and cooked in an imu. *It is said that the jawbone, with the mouth wide open, can be seen to this day at a place by the shore where the waves wash over a rock formation that very much resembles just that.*

People also say that all the ʻalā *stones near where the eel was baked do not crack when heated, as they do elsewhere, because of the heat of that* imu.

It is said that the eelʻs backbone is still lying on the pāhoehoe, *where Aiʻai killed*

Legendary Hawaiian musician Gabby Pahinui, performing at the
1970 Hawaiian Music Festival held in Hāna.

Held in a field across from Hasegawa's Store, the festival attracted
numerous Hawaiian artists and scholars: from left, Auntie Alice
Namakelua, Mary Kawena Pukui and Una Walker.

*it, and on that beach there is, in fact, a rock
formation about 30 feet in length that looks
exactly like the backbone of an eel.*

*The eel's death was a victory for Ai'ai, but
it led to his father's downfall. A protector of
the eel, who came to avenge the death of his
'aumakua, caused Kū-'ula to fall out of favor with the king. The king ordered Kū-'ula,
who had been his head fisherman, to be
burned alive with his family in their home.*

*Kū-'ula told Ai'ai that if the house
burned he must follow the smoke up Ka-iwi-
o-Pele to a cave where he was to live. Then
Kū-'ula handed over his* mana, *his power
over fish, and told Ai'ai to make fishing stations throughout the islands. And so he did.*

The **Hawaiians** utilized a series of
fishing stations in the ocean around the
coast, marking their locations by shore
sightings, a technique invented by Ai'ai.

According to Moke Manu, a Hawaiian

interviewed in Thomas Thrum's *Hawaiian
Annual* of 1902, the first fishing station
where Ai'ai measured the depth of the sea
was where he hooked the eel, a few miles
from the shore to the southeast of the
rocky islet.

The second station that he established
was at a spot about a mile from Hane-o'o
and Hāmoa, which was for the *kala, palani,
pūhi* and *ula,* varieties of fish not caught
by nets or hooks, but in baskets filled with
bait and lowered into the deep sea.

The third station was located in the
ocean at a depth of about 200 fathoms,
close to a sea cave from which the massive
eel launched his attacks on the fishponds.
Fishermen locate the deep sea station by
shore bearings.

In all the stations Ai'ai located there are
no coral ledges where the fishermen's
hooks would catch or the lines be entan-
gled, and old Hawaiians believed that his
skill in this work was due to his father's in-
fluence as an ocean diety.

Paniolo detail, Hana Ranch.

Helicoptering to hidden waterfalls is a special
Hāna Coast experience.

CHAPTER VI

ADVENTURES BEYOND HANA
PAST SEVEN POOLS AND INTO PANIOLO COUNTRY

From Hāna Town the highway moves through two
abandoned villages and into the lowlands of the first of
three geologically important valleys on the south side
of Hale-a-ka-lā: Wai-hoʻi, Wai-lua and Kī-pahulu.

iny Wai-hoʻi Stream was once
a grand waterway, which cut a
valley some 1,800 feet deep
during a period of great erosion. Later, Hāna lavas flooded
it, covering the valley floor to considerable
depth. At the center of this gateway to the
Kī-pahulu area is Wai-o-honu Stream, and
where the stream meets the sea is the village Puʻu-iki, noted since ancient times as
a place of *aliʻi.*

It is said that although the *aliʻi* who settled in Puʻu-iki adopted rural customs and
usually comported themselves as commoners, they acknowledged no authority other
than their own because of their royal blood.

The area is also known as one of the few
places in Hawaiʻi where ancient Hawaiian
artists drew pictographs. Graphic remnants left behind are usually petroglyphs,
etchings in stone. The pictographs are
drawn with red dye on slabs of rock wall
and stylistically feature human figures
with short stubby legs, heavy shoulders,
elongated torsos and long necks.

The western side of Wai-hoʻi Valley is
marked by Papa-hawahawa Stream, which
empties into the sea at Mūʻolea, where
King Ka-lā-kaua maintained a home.

This stretch of the Hāna Coast was one
of the richer areas in ancient times, with
plentiful rain, with valleys ideal for wet-
land farming and with the bountiful sea
close by.

A 1940 issue of *The Hawaiian Planter*
carried a report on the then current agricultural affairs in Wai-lua Valley, noting
that it included the most extensive wet
plantations on the eastern end of Maui:

Altogether, there are about as
many old terraces as at Keanae,
though fewer are now under cultivation. The wet patches at Wailua are at
four levels. Now abandoned are
groups above the [Wailua] falls between the two main streams [Hono-
lewa and Wailua]. Immediately below the falls, behind the small rocky
hill in the center of the valley [at
about where the highway now runs]
is an extensive plantation of well-
watered terraces in which taro flour-
ishes today. At a slightly lower level,
beneath the southwest wall of the
central hill is a group of half a dozen
patches, which were brought back
into cultivation in 1934. In the Valley
bottom, almost at sea level, is the
most extensive area of terraces in
Wailua, extending from the beach to
the mountain and up into the little
valleys on either side. These patches
are no longer used and are covered
with heavy brush and trees.

All along this stretch of the Hāna Coast,
the remnants of farms, villages and *heiau*

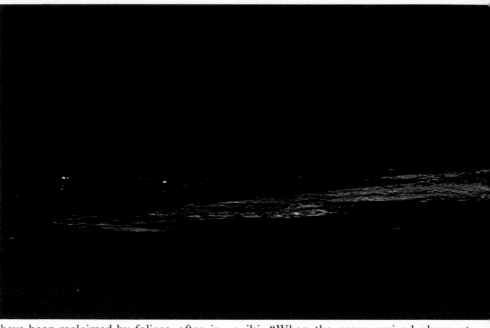

have been reclaimed by foliage, often introduced species, that grows riotously in the fertile, volcanic soil. The brush not only covers the remains but often dislodges the stones used in the original construction, blurring the outlines and making it difficult for any but an expert to discern what was once there.

In modern times, the area from Wai-lua to Kau-pō has become known as a place where nature conspires to keep mankind in one spot, particularly mankind reliant on wheeled vehicles. It rains often and heavily here, turning roads into washes of water and mud cluttered with fallen trees.

In the past it has rained so hard that Hawaiians were able to surf the rivers. Thrum's *Hawaiian Annual* of 1884 described a river surfing scene, reported by travelers who got hit by a downpour just as they arrived at the incline of the cliff of Wai-lua.

The rain extended from Wai-lua to Koali and Mū'olea to the mountain above Pu'u-iki. "When the group arrived above at Pu'u-iki, they saw there was a crowd of people at the stream of Wai-o-honu because the water was flowing heavily. The agitated water was breaking like waves and men and women were surfing on it."

The highway drops back down toward the coast of Pepeiao-lepo Bay near Pua'a-lu'u Stream. There is a story behind those two names.

According to legend Pele was chasing Kama-pua'a, the pig god, after he had ravished her at Hāmoa. With Pele right behind him, Kama-pua'a dove into the stream on the west side of the land and it became known as *pua'a* (pig) *lu'u* (dive). When Kama-pua'a emerged from the bay at the mouth of the stream, his ears were full of mud—hence *pepeiao* (ear) *lepo* (dirty).

In modern times, the fame of Hāna has centered on a string of seven waterfall-fed pools in 'O he'o Gulch. The upper pools are in the Pali-kea Stream which has the help

of the Pīpī-wai Stream in feeding the lower pools.

On January 10, 1969, the secretary of the interior, Stewart Udall, signed documents that made 'Ohe'o and all of Kī-pahulu Valley a part of Hale-a-ka-lā National Park. A coalition of conservationists concerned about the possibility of the area being developed into closed estates had put the property package together and presented it to the federal government. Prime players in that drama included the Nature Conservancy, an organization chartered by the U.S. Congress; Jean and Hamilton Mc-Caughey; and Laurence Rockefeller. The Nature Conservancy raised the funds necessary to purchase the land in the upper Kī-pahulu Valley, while the McCaugheys donated 400 acres at Kū-loa Point (the camping area at the pools) and Rockefeller donated 521 acres at the pools above the highway.

Considering the number of visitors (390,000 in 1985), the facilities at the pools are rudimentary and crowded, largely due to the resistance of Hāna Coast residents to any massive improvements that might stimulate even more traffic. The National Park Service tried to sell the idea of a large development at 'Ohe'o for several years before giving up.

The same sentiment may be the reason the county has failed to substantially improve the potholed road to the pools and beyond, although county officials usually cite the fact there are relatively few residents using the road.

Over the years, the idea grew "Out There" that the pools were somehow sacred, a contention unsupported by any evidence in Hawaiian lore. The idea possibly came from the fact the pools were *kapu* to menstruating women.

According to historian Inez Ashdown, writing in a Maui County publication, the seven pools could be used as a natural rosary by people making the climb up from the sea. (The names of the pools are appar-

"Caution, Baby Pigs Crossing," a painting of roadside Kī-pahulu
by Maui's resident French artist, Guy Buffet.

ently unique with her, as are her translations of the names she uses.)

Those who strived for spiritual ideals would make the trip while praying for help. The pool by the beach is Akakahi, meaning cleansing of all error. The second one, Luakapu, relating to the peace of mind a person enjoys after correcting faults. Next is Ekolu, which begins the pathway to perfection. The fourth is Iolani, meaning the bird of heaven which soars happily. Laulima is the fifth pool and it means removal of all evil and true recognition of good. At Eoana Pool, the lesson is that even good people may be tempted but can overcome evil with proper discipline. The seventh and final pool is Na Hiku and symbolizes the culmination of perfection.

While the pools are the focus of the tourist traffic, the place of real historic value in this extension of Hale-a-ka-lā National Park is Kī-pahulu Valley.

Extremely difficult to reach, Kī-pahulu Valley is one of the few places in all of Hawai'i that has been undisturbed by man. Within its steep walls are flowers, birds and endemic vegetation found nowhere else in the world.

The valley is also of interest to geologists. There are actually two additional stream beds underneath Pali-kea Stream, which runs through the valley. The first cut into the original Honomanū lavas which formed Hale-a-ka-lā and pushed it above the surface of the sea. That bed was filled in by the Hāna flows, which were cut by a second stream. That stream bed was in turn filled by the Kula lava flows now being cut by Pali-kea Stream.

The pools themselves were formed, according to the description of Hawaii scientists Will Kyselka and Ray Lanterman in *Maui: How It Came to Be,* by swift flowing water "bouncing off rock walls, turning in-

Local Kī-pahulu folks, Joe and Annie Kahaleuahi.

Hui-aloha Church, 1922.

'A Gathering of Love'

America was preparing to celebrate its bicentennial birthday and from Washington D.C., word had come that on July 4th every church bell in the nation was to be rung in unison.

The bell at Hui-aloha Church had been frozen so long that no one in Kau-pō could remember the last time they had heard it. The church was still used occasionally, but the steeple was riddled with dry-rot and termites and, along with the rest of the historic structure, was badly in need of repair.

We were there to make a short film to be used in raising funds to help with the rebuilding. With us were two Hawaiian women, Alice Apo and Daisy Kekoanui. Now well into their seventies, both remembered attending church here when there were so many people in the congregation that two services were held every Sunday, each so crowded that they, along with the other children, were made to stand outside.

On an impulse we decided that our sound track could not be complete without the pealing of the bell, so two of us decided to give it a try. The climb up was dark and frightening, and finding timbers strong enough to serve as foot- and hand-holds an arduous challenge.

Reaching the bell, we took opposite sides of the badly rusted pulley, alternately pushing and pulling down in an effort to break it loose. It moved a little, then a little more, and, suddenly, with a great crunching sound, it gave, and the bell rang out, echoing back from the hills outside. It was as if life had returned to Hui-aloha.

We gathered in a small circle to hold hands and *pule*, offer a prayer—like the very name of the church, Hui-aloha, "A Gathering of Love." The room was filled with memories, and we wept for them.

—Carl Lindquist

Hawaiian headstone at Hui-aloha Church's cemetery.

side out, churning and eddying, wearing away at the fracture and jointing planes."

The land on the south side of the 'Ohe'o Gulch has historically been a rich agricultural place, worked first by the Hawaiians and later by sugar planters and cattle ranchers.

The area has also become known in recent times for the secluded estates of the rich and the famous, who have settled on the Hāna Coast, enjoying its beauty and, even more, its relative isolation and privacy.

A smokestack and a group of abandoned concrete structures on the upper side of the road mark the Kipahulu Sugar Mill. The areas of the coast beyond this point were reachable only by foot or mule until the 1930s, when a crew hired by the federal government turned what was left of the old Hawaiian foot highway into something a wheeled vehicle could traverse.

In the early part of this century, the area supported many small villages, accounting for the churches which are scattered in a now seemingly senseless pattern across the countryside from Kī-pahulu to Kau-pō.

The road along this stretch of the coast often clings perilously to wave-pounded cliffs. A major storm in 1980, followed by another in 1982, closed the road when heavy rains washed the cliffs down onto the roads.

At its best, the road between Hāna and Kau-pō is just passable; the question of whether or not it is open is a daily issue determined, on the one hand, by weather and, on the other, by the stamina of county supervisor Bill-John Medeiros's overworked road crews.

At Kukui Bay, an old trail leads down to Puhi-lele (Leaping Eel) Point and a collection of abandoned house and work sites— what is now left of a one-time thriving community of Chinese peanut farmers.

One of the last *ahupua'a* in the Kī-pahulu district is called Kukui-'ula, a place

which gave rise to a ghost story and is thought to be named after it.

Kukui-'ula is said to be the name of a woman who lived in the area with her husband. When she died he buried his beloved wife near the house and erected a shrine over the grave. One night when the moon was full, he sat by the shrine. A figure arose from the shrine and asked for one of the children. The man was delighted by what he assumed was his wife's return to him, and ran to get their youngest child. She ate the child, and asked for another.

Realizing that he was dealing with a demon, the man gave her the oldest child and ran with the middle child for help. His sister fought the demon, while the man and his remaining son raced for the protection of a kahuna, *a priest, at a* heiau *near Hāmoa.*

One of the most important installations in any given area in the old days was the *pu'uhonua,* or place of refuge, usually a *heiau* where anyone could find sanctuary—from the wrath of a chief, a priest, a neighbor or even a demon.

One such *pu'uhonua* was the Pōpō-iwi Heiau constructed by Ke-kaulike in about 1730 on a hill that is on the right side of the road as it climbs up a ramp-like incline straight north of Hui-aloha Church, a restored Congregationlist "circuit" church originally constructed in 1859. Kau-pō was then a landlocked community except for the rough trails and the path through the gap and crater.

The first detailed descriptions of this section of the coast written by western man were entries in the journal of the French explorer La Pérouse. During an around-the-world voyage of exploration and scientific investigation for Louis XVI of France, La Pérouse's two-ship fleet sighted Maui on May 28, 1786, from the south.

The Moku-lau Peninsula, Kau-pō.

As he sailed along the Kī-pahulu coast he noted in a journal:

> Water cascades from the mountain tops, irrigating the native villages before it enters the sea. The dwellings are so numerous that a single village extends for three or four leagues. All the houses are at the edge of the sea, and the mountains are so near that the habitable land does not appear to be more than a quarter league wide.

La Pérouse sailed along the Kau-pō and Ka-naio Coast, looking for both an anchorage and a source of water, but was unable to land due to rough seas battering the rugged coast.

As the ships *Boussole* and *Astrolabe* beat down the coast, La Pérouse observed a great fleet of canoes being paddled furiously and unsuccessfully in an effort to catch the French transports. La Pérouse wrote that about 50 of the canoes were capsized and swamped in the chase down the coast.

He noted that being dumped into the sea didn't seem to bother the Hawaiians much since they "are such good swimmers that they stand comparison with seals and sea lions."

La Pérouse finally anchored at the bay which was then called Ke-one-'ō'io and later renamed for the explorer. The Hawaiians and the French had both heard about Capt. James Cook's visit and untimely end but the nervous Frenchmen were greeted with characteristic hospitality. While trading, La Pérouse was given a pig by two men who seemed to be in authority and, in return, he gave them iron implements.

In his journal, he described the village as numbering 10 to 15 huts—

> . . . made of grass and covered with the same material. They have the same shape as the thatched cottages

found in certain parts of France. The roofs are pitched on two sides and the door, which is located on the gable end, is only three feet high, so that it is necessary to stoop when entering.

The furnishings consist of mats which, like our carpets, make a very neat flooring on which the islanders sleep. The only cooking utensils they have are gourds painted in various colors.

When he returned to the ship, La Pérouse found his executive officer had received a chief on board and had acquired a feather cape and helmet as well as a great many provisions, including bananas, yams, taro and more than a hundred pigs. That night, the Frenchman sailed west, by Moloka'i, and on out into the Pacific. He was lost when his ships wrecked on a reef near Fiji but his journals survived, having been sent home before his fatal South Pacific wreck.

One of the tasks set for La Pérouse was verification of Spanish charts then in existence. The Spanish were notorious for doctoring charts to keep their discoveries secret. However, there is an impressive body of circumstantial evidence which indicates that the Spanish visited Hawai'i well in advance of Cook or La Pérouse.

This evidence includes the style of the Hawaiian helmets and capes, which matches the design and color of the raiment of Spanish nobles of the 1600s; the fact the Spanish were crossing the Pacific from the Americas to the Philippines for 200 years before Cook; the appearance of white-skinned people in the oral traditions of the islands; and, most of all, a Spanish chart dated 1555.

The chart was drawn by Juan Gaetano and shows a group of islands in the same latitude occupied by the Hawaiian islands and with a longitude that is off by only about 10 degrees.

Gaetano identified what appears to be

Christian Hedemann with horses and buggy,
Kī-pahulu Plantation, ca. 1880s.

Maui as La Desgradiada, which means "The Unfortunate." That would be an apt description if the Spaniard saw Maui from the south during one of the periodic droughts that hit the area between Kau-pō and the normally dry regions the Hawaiians call the Ka-naio Coast.

Between the time of Cook's second visit to Maui and La Pérouse's short stopover, Ka-mehameha the Great came to power on the Big Island. Among his forays into Ka-hekili's kingdom were battles at Kau-pō where it was traditional in the Maui/Big Island struggles to first establish a beachhead and then move overland through Kī-pahulu and on to Hāna.

Except for those occasions when politics brought war to the region, Kau-pō was a place of farmers.

Traveling from Kī-pahulu, the road now crosses a modern concrete bridge spanning the seaward reaches of Mana-wai-nui Stream, which runs out of the amphithea-ter-like Mana-wai-nui Canyon. Despite the enormous amount of water caught in the canyon, the ground is so porous that Mana-wai-nui Stream is often dry. Many of the ancient villages that dotted this area of the coast were built around the rocky mouths of gulches, leaving the best land free for farming. It must have been exciting when the Kona storms came and filled the gulches with raging torrents.

In addition to being a farming area for dry-land crops, and a transit for conquerors and defenders, until Kiha-a-pi'ilani's foot highway was built, Kau-pō was famous for its robbers.

In 1910 the *Pacific Commercial Advertiser* ran a series of reports from Kau-pō that indicated the area was "a kind of jumping off place, but is a most interesting settlement and if a road were built along the beach would attract tourists."

That road remains unbuilt and would likely be greeted with something less than enthusiasm on the part of modern day Kau-

St. Joseph's Catholic Church, Kau-pō.

Branding time, 'Ulu-pala-kua Ranch.

pō residents. These are a people who prize their isolation and a lifestyle that owes more to the past than the present.

Those 1910 reports also indicate that Kau-pō was an area that grew limes and oranges, a commercial venture that existed at the whim of the interisland steamers. One article tells about limes and oranges rotting at Moku-lau Landing and the residents being reduced to famine rations for lack of supplies because the ship had not shown up.

In modern times, the isolation at Kau-pō depends largely on the condition of the road. The schoolhouse at Kau-pō Village was re-opened in 1982 when the road to Hāna was cut by storms and landslides.

For a time after the storm, the area was cut off totally from the outside, but now Civil Defense officials have installed a radio link between Kaupo Ranch and emergency agencies.

Except when Kona storms rake the peninsula with wind-driven rain, the weather at Kau-pō tends to be dry, with the greenery of hardy *kiawe* and brush turned dull by the dust kicked up by passing vehicles, plodding cattle and the omnipresent wind.

It wasn't always that way.

Until the 1930s, several large, copious springs in Mana-wai-nui Valley provided ample supplies of irrigation water. Landslides caused by heavy rains, earthquakes and generally unstable conditions of the sheer walls of the valley covered the springs, and broke the pipelines, cutting the water availability drastically.

In 1921 the peninsula was described by Thomas Manapau who had accompanied Dr. Kenneth P. Emory of the Bishop Museum on a trip to Kau-pō:

"Kau-pō is indeed a green land and so is Hāna. They look so open and pleasant to live in because the wind is always blowing."

During their visit, Manapau and Emory apparently made the acquaintance of a

Kaupo Store, 1983: a morning scene.

Kau-pō bard who told them of the local winds:

Moae winds [trades,] are the customary winds that blow strongly but pleasantly from the sea and sometimes from the land. It is sung about: 'Where are you, O *moae* wind/You're taking my love with you.'

Moae-ku [strong trades] is like the *moae* but much stronger. This wind is said to have been born in Hāna, grew up in Kipahulu, attained maturity in Kaupo, became aged in Kahikinui, grew feeble at Kanaio, rested and let its burden down at Honoaula. Here is a song for this wind: 'Where are you, O *Moae-ku*/You make much work on a stormy day.'

Kulene [possibly gusty] wind comes with rain. It blows strongly out to sea from the land.

Kaomi [to press down] is a strong, blustering wind whose strength does not last long but blows with a gentle pressure. It is sung thus: 'The wind blows in a gale,/Then it gently presses.'

Kiu [moderately cold out of the northwest] is a wind that flies along and seems to sneak by to the mountain of Haleakala. Here is a song of this wind: 'The *kiu* is the wind that lives in the mountains.'

Naulu [sudden shower]. This wind goes with the *naulu* clouds: 'The *naulu* is the wind/It bears the *naulu* clouds along.'

Makani kaili aloha o Kipahulu. The love-snatching-wind-of-Kipahulu is the usual Kipahulu wind. It blows down from the mountain and goes out to sea.

(Reprinted from Maui: How It Came to Be *by Will Kyselka and Ray Lanterman, University Press of Hawaii, 1980.)*

Kipahulu Store, 1921: (from left) George Soon, Sam Soon, Hāna
Sheriff Levi Joseph and Philip Soon.

Kau-pō Village today is a scattered collection of homes occupied by families who have always lived on the coast and by other families who have moved here in recent times in an effort to establish self-sufficiency. They've met with varying degrees of success, many having been drawn to the peninsula as much by the relatively low prices of land as the place itself. Water appears to be a very large problem.

At the center of the village is the Kaupo Store, the last of the string of stores operated by the Soon family that once stretched from Ke-'anae to Kau-pō. The store in Kau-pō is open on an irregular schedule and serves as a miniature museum of memorabilia from the days when Nick Soon brought in the first Model T in pieces by barge and assembled the first electric generator on the peninsula. The senior Mr. Soon also happened to be an inveterate photographer, and became known as Kau-pō's answer to Thomas Alva Edison.

The store is a regular stop for hikers coming out of the crater, down the Kau-pō Gap.

The unexpected becomes the expected on this part of the Hāna Coast. A driver might come across a herd of russet-colored thoroughbred steers being driven along the dusty white gravel road. When that happens there is really nothing to do but wait.

A few years ago, when the road was rough but passable, it was common for tour vans to make the circuit of East Maui. The nine-passenger vans often traveled in two- or three-vehicle convoys. One day, a convoy of three was faced with a dilemma.

The drivers had to keep more or less to schedule but found the road filled with huge, if amiable animals. They pulled the vans slowly into the herd and were stopped by the sheer mass of meat. The tourists inside the vans were excited and seemed to be enjoying the experience until the animals started pushing against the sides of the

Kau-pō Gap: the passageway for the massive lava flow
that formed Kau-pō.

. . . And Out Kau-po Gap

The best way to make the hike out of the crater by way of Kau-pō Gap is in two stages.

The first stage is the easier of the two, down the old Hawaiian foot trails carved in the sides of the steep places and meandering paths through a series of three plateaus.

Both stages are less than a half-day's effort when the weather is good, which for the hiker usually means sunshine. A short hike means more time to dawdle over breakfast, striking the tent and getting the gear together.

The campsite at Pali-kū is the "wet" end of the crater but there hasn't been any appreciable rain for some time. The other campers are either staying put or heading back toward the other side of the crater. It will be a quiet walk down to the ranch and the village.

The gap is a beautiful place, its lushness heightened by the arid, red-brown that characterizes the crater floor. The three steps down the top part of the gap are separated by drop-offs.

Here there is a temptation to strike off on your own, leaving the narrow foot trail to others. It's a temptation held in check by the frequent stories of individuals getting hopelessly lost in terrain that twists with gullies and sheer *pali,* cliffs softened by growths of plants only a trained botanist could identify.

At the top of the trail down to Kau-pō, the land is an undulation of hummocks, grass-covered and spiked with a plethora of ferns and low bush-type plants.

And ahead . . .

A lift of the eyes lays the entire downward sweep of the gap at your feet. There is blue of the sky above and the blue of the ocean below. The Kula Volcanic Series lava walls of the gap conspire in an optical illusion for the hiker, a fore-shortening that makes it seem almost as if you can reach out and touch Kau-pō Village, more than eight miles away and 1200 feet below.

The trail stays mostly on the Kī-pahulu side

of the gap. In places where the later Hāna Volcanic Series lava floor of the gap falls away over *pali* 50 to 60 feet high and higher, the walking is the easiest. Trails are cut into the side of the *pali*, switching back and forth, ducking under guavas and other trees, bending around boulders that got left behind when all of this was a rushing sea of mud.

Everywhere you look, to the sides, up at the walls of the gap, down to the sea, there is something to charm and delight.

It's easy to imagine small groups of Hawaiians walking this way, up and down, on trading missions and in war parties. It's a little harder to imagine herds of cattle being driven this way, down the gap after a trip up to and through the crater, but that was done once, too.

The first half of the hike out Kau-pō ends at a huge *koa* tree planted securely in the side of the gap and making a natural camping spot— unsanctioned by anything but tradition. Just below is the water tank that is part of the Kau-

pō Ranch/Village water system. This marks the start of the rough part of the walk out of Kau-pō—a jeep road that runs mostly up and down in a grade that is guaranteed to weary those who are fit and bring tears to the eyes of those who aren't. It's this steep, rocky road that focuses all of the hiker's weight on straining knees and toes jamming into the fronts of boots that makes over-nighting "at the tree" an advisable precaution.

At morning, Kau-pō has disappeared. The view extends less than 10 yards in a billow of white-grey clouds. Moisture drips off everything. The small butane stove heats the water necessary for a breakfast brew of cocoa and instant coffee. All of the gear gets packed and the walk into the cloud begins. Dry, the jeep road is rugged enough to lame; wet, it's a kind of passive antagonist. It's wet today and gets wetter.

The four miles down to the village grows longer, marching, sliding, slipping down the rocky road. Occasional excursions across switchbacks are greeted with toe stubbing rocks and even worse conditions than the road itself. Soaked boots gnaw at tenderized flesh. The pace slows. Off in the distance, the ranch dogs bark at something.

Minds become as leaden as the skies. There is no real rain now, just a weepy kind of wetness that soaks more thoroughly than immersion.

The hike becomes a walk through a primal place of banana trees and vines as the trail swings around the upper portion of the ranch buildings, and goes over fences on wooden steps built and maintained by the ranch.

The trail head is almost on the front steps of the ranch office, with gates closing off the property. It's a good place to sit even out in the rain. The butane stove is going. Hot coffee helps.

—R.Y.

Round-up time, ʻUlu-pala-kua.

vans, rocking the heavy vehicles from side to side.

The Kau-pō paniolo *kept the herd moving around the vans but didn't do anything to hurry the animals beyond the normal pace. The* paniolo *faces under sweat-stained hats were impassive even when the tourists' eyes began popping. There was a feeling of laughter in the air.*

Anything might appear on the road that tunnels through the *kiawe* and old citrus trees on the Kau-pō Peninsula. About a quarter mile beyond the abandoned St. Joseph's Catholic Church there is a rough jeep trail angling down to Ka-mana-wai Bay and Ka-ʻīlio Point. The point is interesting historically and geologically.

One of the first battles between Ka-lani-ʻōpuʻu and Ka-hekili took place here. The forces of Ka-hekili successfully repelled the Big Islanders, who included a young warrior named Ka-mehameha.

Sitting astride Ka-ʻīlio Point is a 75-foot hill with a limestone layer more than a foot thick capping it. On it are shells of a marine gastropod, *Littorina.* The cap is not part of an ancient emerged reef; it is actually still forming today as sea snails climb the point and their shells are incorporated into the limestone.

Continuing up on the coast route, the traveler is now on a road constructed by prison labor in the 1950s.

Across from Waiū ("Female Breast") Bay is Puʻu Māneʻoneʻo, ("Itchy Hill"). The hill is actually the result of a massive mudslide set into motion up in the gap by earthquakes, carrying down everything that was moveable, only to end in a heap here.

Nuʻu was once an important cattle shipping port, partly for those herds brought across the mountain through the Kau-pō Gap, and was also a place where salt was gathered. The Hawaiians dug shallow "pans" in the boulders to trap sea water. The sun and time did most of the rest of the work.

Beyond Nuʻu, the road begins a gentle climb up the face of the mountain, running inland and affording transcendental views both up and down and across the slope. This is Maui's largest desert area. The land is scrubby, littered with ʻaʻā lava and almost without any natural sources of water. It is open range, mostly owned by the state and leased by ranches or livestock operations.

The cattle pastured here are wiry, semi-wild creatures, sharing the land's meager bounty with goats, descended from animals originally left in the islands by Cook and other early sea captains looking for a mid-Pacific source of meat for their crews.

At the time of Cook there were hundreds of Hawaiians living in this area. It is said that farming was done by digging holes in the rocks and filling them with dirt carried in from other locations. Today it is hard to imagine the area as a once flourishing agricultural area but it must be remembered that this was before the 1790 explosion of lava out of two vents above La Pérouse Bay. It was also well before the destruction of the upper level forests by cattle and goats. Before the turn of this century, the forests on Ka-hoʻolawe, an off-shore island that has been denuded by goats and blasted by U.S. Navy training bombardments, caught the clouds and in the afternoon sent them back across the channel to ʻUlu-pala-kua. There they gathered on the tree-filled upper slopes of this now desolate coast.

Between Nuʻu and the Lualaʻi-lua Hills was a large agricultural settlement known as Kahiki-nui, "Great Tahiti". The farmers here worked on terraced land and built a collection of homesteads, burial sites, animal pens, storage caves and heiau platforms.

In the area makai of the current highway, haole farmers once tried to grow wheat. Farther down, on the coast, are some of the most vivid remains of the pre-Cook Hawaiian lifestyle: an ancient foot highway. The Nuʻu end of the foot highway is discernable only in outline. This end of the area has enough grass growing to disrupt the mortarless paving. Years of running cattle in the area and the wheat farming efforts also did their share to obliterate the old pathway, and some of the paving ended up in rock walls built to restrain cattle.

But, in the lava flows, the highway lies ready to serve and to remind one of an older time. The La Pérouse end of the foot highway is reached by a foot path, marked primarily by faint scuff marks in the ʻaʻā lava. The hike along the foot highway, from La Pérouse to Nuʻu, takes most of three days. There are only two water sources, both close to the La Pérouse end: a cattle trough that may or may not be hooked up on any given day and some brackish springs that provide drinkable if unsavory water.

It's a strange sensation to walk along the chipped rock paving that undulates slightly across gullies that have been built up and on finger-ridges of lava that have been smoothed over. The small rock of the paving is held in place by walls of rock along the sides, a kind of curbing. The foot highway is about four feet wide and runs straight across the lava, ignoring the twists and turns of the rocky, high-bluff coastline, in a perfect east-west alignment, obviously taken from the sun's summer transit.

One of the best preserved traditional Hawaiian settlements is a few hours' walk down the foot highway and is marked by house sites set almost a perfect half-day's walk apart. The village is a cattle feeding site for ʻUlu-pala-kua Ranch, which has forced a four-wheel-drive trail down from the upper road, and the last available water (if the line is turned on) until Nuʻu, a long day's walk over the lower slopes.

Herding cattle in rangelands above ʻUlu-pala-kua.

The upper road, Piʻi-lani Highway, moves ever uphill toward the ridge that runs down from the top and terminates in Kīhei. In dry times, the lava is flat and listless. After a rain, though, the black rock is studded with yellow poppies and the blue, red and yellow of lantana. The highway cuts below the old ranch village of Ka-naio ("Bastard Sandalwood Tree"), which survived into modern times as a home for *paniolo* and their families. Some of the old houses have been adopted by newcomers unconcerned about the lack of civilized amenities. Although in very recent times it appears someone has tried to link Ka-naio with the highway via a bulldozer track, the main road to this village only yards away from the road is miles down the highway, close to an intersection with the road down to Mākena.

Just past the turnoff to Ka-naio, the highway runs through the beginnings of forest lands and into ʻUlu-pala-kua ("Breadfruit Ripening on the Backs of Carriers"). In the old days, it must have been a long journey, indeed.

The isolation here on the face of the last active rift zone of Hale-a-ka-lā has led ʻUlu-pala-kua Ranch and its predecessors to a colorful share of Hawaii history.

The 30,000-acre ʻUlu-pala-kua Ranch is a cattle/sheep/vineyard/real estate operation that is still more ranch than anything else under the management of C. Pardee Erdman.

The ranch stretches from the 6,500-foot level of the mountain down to the coast and includes vast strips of land immediately behind the developed areas of Kīhei.

ʻUlu-pala-kua Ranch is the landlord from Mākena to Kīhei and has played big roles in the development of Mākena. That is the big money part of ʻUlu-pala-kua Ranch. The romantic part is up the hill in the well-worn saddles of tradition-garlanded *paniolo*.

The senior hand on the ranch is Kauhi

Kauhi Purdy, *paniolo.*

Purdy, son of world champion cowboy Ikua Purdy who won his titles early this century at Cheyenne, Wyoming, and Pendleton, Oregon. The life of the cowboy at ʻUlu-pala-kua has changed little since he began ranching here during the last century.

The early glory of the area is due to a whaling ship captain who was nearly killed by a crewman with a hatchet.

J ames Makee was master of the whaling ship *Maine* in 1843 when he was attacked in his sleep. The steward who wielded the hatchet was so amazed when Makee got up anyway, blood streaming from his head, he jumped overboard.

Makee quit the sea after that incident and purchased what would become Rose Ranch in 1856. At that time, the principal business was sugar cane. Makee built a mill near the center of today's ranch to grind the sugar that provided handsome profits—until the weather changed drastically with a drought in 1877. The last sugar crop was

ground at the mill in 1883 and taken down the road to Mākena Landing for loading on ships.

Makee was a high roller. He built a showplace house (burned down in recent times) and was known far and wide as a generous host. Guests included King Kalā-kaua, who used the occasion of the first voyage of the S. S. *Kilauea,* the first steamship on the interisland line, to visit Rose Ranch.

For that visit Makee rolled out the royal carpet to the extent of organizing a 150-horseman greeting at Mākena Landing and a torch-light procession that traversed the entire five miles up to the ranch house.

A three-day party ensued. The festivities were described by a member of the royal entourage as being on "a princely scale of hospitality."

Makee's parties were famous and his specialty was hosting ranking officers off the warships that occasionally anchored at Mākena Landing. The usual Makee party

Sunset light over 'Ulu-pala-kua.

would include a roast peacock entree, and his house was filled with cut flowers, pine sprays and *maile.*

He was also a sporting man who enjoyed a game of cards, a pastime that King Ka-lā-kaua also indulged in.

As one story goes, Makee once thought he had won the island of Molo-kini, a cres-cent-shaped islet in the channel between Maui and Ka-ho'olawe. It happened on the occasion of the visit King Ka-lā-kaua made on the S. S. *Kilauea.* The king was not holding good cards and had gambled away his last chip. But, he called for one more hand, offering Molo-kini in a game of showdown. Makee won and expressed delight over owning the island. "Molo-kini?" countered the monarch. "I didn't bet Molo-kini; I wagered *'ōmole kini,* a bottle of gin."

Rose Ranch got its name from the roses Makee had planted on the terraced gardens around his house. After the end of the sugar planting industry, the property was devoted to raising cattle and was super-vised by a top hand imported from the Big Island's last Parker Ranch.

That hand was Ikua Purdy, father of Kauhi, grandfather of Dan and George, great-grandfather of Myron and Byron and spiritual father of four generations of Ha-waiian cowboys.

The Rose Ranch, after Makee's death in 1879, continued the tradition of hospi-tality. During the early years of the 20th Century, it hosted Sun Yat Sen. His family stayed there while Sun Yat Sen organized and fought the revolution in China against the Manchu warlords. Sun Yat Sen is con-sidered to be the George Washington of China, even by the Communists.

In 1963, the 30,000 acres that made up 'Ulu-pala-kua Ranch passed into the hands of its current owner, C. Pardee Erdman. The price was $3.5 million. The property stretched from the sea at Mākena to the 6,500-foot level of Hale-a-ka-lā and ecom-

Near harvest time in 'Ulu-pala-kua's Tedeschi Vineyard.

passed every type of landscape and vegetation found on the island.

Although Erdman once turned down $25 million in cash for the ranch, he is more like a corporate executive than a simple rancher.

At a time when cattle ranches throughout the United States were going out of business, Erdman raised cash by selling real estate, including a 1,000-acre parcel at Mākena for $7.5 million. He shrugged off those who complained about his selling one of Maui's last undeveloped beachfront areas to Seibu Hawaii, Inc., with the comment that "I don't think the future of this land is in large-scale cattle raising."

Erdman is a Princeton graduate whose studies of agriculture and geology have borne fruit in creative diversification at 'Ulu-pala-kua. He introduced sheep in the island meat market and is working with Maui Electric Co. to develop geothermal wells in the arid land near the island's most recent lava flow. In addition, he is support-

ing the first serious attempt to produce a Hawaiian wine.

California vintner Emil Tedeschi took over a section of 'Ulu-pala-kua's range to develop a Maui vineyard. While the experiments with different types of grapes were being conducted and the first vines planted and brought to maturity, Tedeschi developed a truly local wine that pleases some and amuses others. Using a pineapple base, Tedeschi produced *Maui Blanc*, a still sweet wine, later adding a pineapple based sparkling wine. A beaujolais wine and a natural champagne have also been added. The Tedeschis' tasting room is in the ranch's old milk house, across the road from the remains of Makee's sugar mill.

Nevertheless, it is the cattle that make 'Ulu-pala-kua what it is today, a place of sprawling pastures, open skies and the gentle rhythms of man and horse against cattle and terrain.

Weekend rodeos are held several times a year in the ranch arena. It is a favorite spot

On the trail, Hale-a-ka-lā.

Science City.

for the Maui Cowgirls Association to stage events, and junior rodeo riders regularly pit their skill against the animals there.

And it is still possible to be driving along the undulating highway through 'Ulu-pala-kua and to see, as if rising from the ground itself, a herd of cattle being mosied over the next rise by straight-backed cowboys.

'Ulu-pala-kua Ranch lies astride the southwest rift of the Hale-a-ka-lā Volcano, a spine-like ridge that runs up this flank of the mountain to the cloud-shrouded top.

Near the upper limits of the ranch land is Polipoli State Park and the man-planted Polipoli State Forest preserve, a place where pine trees grow in strange and marvelous ways due to the ebb and flow of the moisture-laden clouds.

Barring wings, the best way to get to Polipoli State Park from 'Ulu-pala-kua is to drive away from the Hāna Coast into Kula and up Waipoli Road, a convict-built track

paved only partway and a challenge to the hardiest of off-road vehicles.

Camping is permitted at the park, with permits obtainable in Wai-luku. It's possible to hike up from the park to the top of the mountain, although the walk is usually done from the top, down.

The ridge line is edged by a trail that is closed to vehicles to keep dust from complicating the lives of scientists working in Hale-a-ka-lā's Science City.

It's a fascinating walk, with the mountain falling away on all sides and grassy slopes checkered with pheasant, chukkas and Franklin Quail.

Coming up from the bottom, the hiker moves through the clouds and finally emerges at Science City, a high-tech aggregation of observatories and tracking stations and communication facilities. Perched on the edge, but outside of Hale-a-ka-lā National Park, Science City began in 1956 when the University of Hawaii, which operates the overall facility, set up a satel-

The Hawaiian *nēnē*
goose, Hale-a-ka-lā.

lite tracking station using a telescope borrowed from New Mexico.

In later years, the unpolluted atmosphere of the 10,000-foot summit and its accessibility made it a popular site for star gazing, solar studies and military operations. In addition to traditional telescopes, the 18 acres at Science City include lasers for tracking satellites. During the first flight of the space shuttle *Columbia,* an electro-optical telescope on Hale-a-ka-lā took pictures of the ship's heat tiles.

Construction of the latest facility at Science City, put in by the Air Force, stirred the ire of environmentalists.

According to Hale-a-ka-lā National Park superintendent Hugo Huntzinger, the Air Force agreed to cooperate short of relocating the facility entirely. "If all this were occurring 25 or 30 years ago and we had the laws we have now, Science City wouldn't exist as it does today," Huntzinger said, adding he was primarily concerned with visual pollution from the building and the facility's trash attracting mongooses and rats which, in turn, would prey on the endangered Dark Rumped Petrel which nests in burrows on the top of the mountain.

After moving through Science City, a hiker can go on up to the edge of the crater rim at Pakao'ao Cone, one of three cinder cones atop Hale-a-ka-lā. The others are Red Hill, at the very top, and Magnetic Peak, an iron-ore rich mound named for its power over a compass.

The name Hale-a-ka-lā generally describes the entire mountain, from shore to summit, yet it is most properly applied to a peak on the west side of Kau-pō Gap.

According to the ancients, a demi-god named Māui once stood on that peak, armed with a net and determined to do battle with the sun as it streaked across the sky.

As related through the generations, Māui's mother, Hina, was having great difficulty drying her fine kapa. *The days were too short. The sun raced overhead too quickly. There was, in fact, so much darkness that the leaves were pressed flat on all the trees.*

Māui watched the sun moving across the sky and made his plan to correct the situation. He wove a net from the 'ie'ie *vine and the* olonā *shrub. With the net, he crept up the side of Kau-pō Gap so as to be in position when Lā, the sun, whipped up through the gap and across the sky.*

As the sun sped into the sky, Māui threw his net and snared Lā. Māui held firm against Lā's struggles, and the two struck a bargain. Māui would release the sun if he promised to move more slowly across the sky. Lā agreed. And it was so. The sun moved slowly across the sky, making each day longer and warmer.

And that is the most famous adventure of them all—On the Hāna Coast.

A fine Hale-a-ka-lā silversword in full bloom.

CHAPTER VII

GUIDELINES AND MAPS

How to Get There

By Plane To Ka-hului: There are four airlines with regular flights from Honolulu to Ka-hului — **Aloha Airlines, Hawaiian Airlines, Mid Pacific Airlines** and **Princeville Airways** — and other carriers that fly directly to Ka-hului from destinations on the mainland — **United Airlines, American Airlines** and **Western Airlines.**

By Plane To Hāna: Only Princeville Airways maintains a regular schedule directly into Hāna, offering several flights daily from locations throughout the islands. Scenic fly-drive tours are offered from Ka-hului to Hāna by **Maui Helicopters** [phone (808) 879-1601] and charter flights by **Paragon Air** [phone (808) 871-7622]. Both connect with ground tours in Hāna. (See *Things To Do*.)

By Tour Van: The following companies offer one-day tours of the Hāna Coast. Advance reservations are required in most cases, and may be made after arriving on Maui.

Akami Tours will pick up from locations in Kapa-lua, Kīhei, Maalaea, Wai-lea and Ka-hului. It leaves 7-Pools at 3 p.m. for the return trip. [P.O. Box 395, Ka-hului, Maui, HI 96732]

Ekahi Tours, Inc., will pick up from locations in Kapa-lua, Napili, Kāana-pali, Lahaina, Mākena, Kīhei, Maalaea, and Ka-hului. Lunch is at the Hāna Ranch restaurant. [205 Puka-lani, Puka-lani, Maui, HI 96768]

Grayline-Maui will pick up from locations in Kāʻana-pali, Wai-Lea, Na-pili and Kapa-lua *only*. [273 Dairy Rd., Ka-hului, Maui, HI 96732; (toll free) (800) 367-2420, (on Maui) (808) 877-5507]

Na Ka Oi Scenic Tours, Inc., will pick up from locations in Kapa-lua, Kāʻana-pali, Lahaina, Wai-Lea, Suda Store, Kīhei and Ka-hului. It includes lunch and visits to 7-Pools and Lindbergh's grave. Departs Hāna 3-3:30 p.m. [531 S. Papa Ave., P.O. Box 1827, Ka-hului, Maui, HI 96732 ... phone (808) 871-9008]

Robert's Hawaii, Inc., will pick up from all hotels and condominiums on the islands. [430 Hāna Highway, P.O. Box 1563, Ka-hului, Maui, HI 96732 ... (808) 871-6226]

Trans Hawaiian Maui will pick up from any point on Maui between 6:30 and 7:45 a.m. Excursions run every day to Hāna, returning from Hāna between 3 and 3:30 p.m. [845 Palapala Dr., Ka-hului, Maui, HI 96732 ... (808) 877-7308]

Tropical Excursions leaves West Maui between 6:30 and 7 a.m. Breakfast at Pāʻia. Departs Hāna between 12:30 and 1 p.m. Operates six to seven days a week. [P.O. Box 597, Pāʻia, Maui, HI 96779 ... (808) 579-8422]

By Car: There are myriad rental and leasing companies operating out of booths in the Ka-hului Airport and from offices downtown. If you are interested in driving on the unpaved section of the Hāna Coast near Kau-pō, you would be well advised to check with the rental car company in advance.

Stopping in Pāʻia

The best way to drive to Hāna, particularly if you plan to drive back again the same day, is to begin early, stopping for breakfast in one of the little restaurants in Pāʻia, the "Last Chance" watering hole before

Hāna Town.

You can also pick up a picnic lunch to enjoy at one of the breathtaking parks along the way. Up from the highway on Baldwin Avenue, **Picnics** packs lunches and offers a light breakfast of pastry and coffee while you wait. You can also order a lunch in advance. [30 Baldwin Avenue, Pā'ia, HI 96779 . . . phone (808) 579-8021]

The alternative is to pick up your own lunch — anything from real manapua to fresh fruit, cheese and screw top wine — in one of the small Mom & Pop grocery stores in town.

Whatever else you do, don't leave Pā'ia with less than a full tank of gas. Hāna Highway is dotted with tempting side trips, and there isn't another gas station until Hāna Town.

On the Road to Hāna

There are countless gems on the road to Hāna, and every state park on the way is worthy of a visit. There are a few other lovely stops a Hāna Highway novice might miss:

Ke-'anae Arboretum is simply identified by a sign saying "The Arboretum" on the highway just past Honomanū Bay. It is a great picnic spot, even though there are no rest room facilities, and a beautiful place to take pictures. There are plants from all over the world in the arboretum, and many of them have grown to awesome sizes. (There are elephant's ears so large that people standing beside them look like midgets.)

Ke-'anae Peninsula, with its old stone church, emerald taro fields and black lava rock coastline, is a wonderful side trip, too. It can be reached by car on a half-mile dirt road that winds down the mountain and onto the promontory.

Shortly after the peninsula turn off is the **Wai-lua Valley Lookout,** where you can stretch your legs and take in a view of the valley and the peninsula.

And if you didn't stock up on enough food for the road in Pā'ia, the relatively new **Wai-anu Fruit Stand,** noted for home-baked goodies and fresh fruit juice, is about a quarter mile past the arboretum.

A mile before Hāna Town is **Helani Gardens,** nearly 60 acres of lushly landscaped grounds, owned by Howard F. Cooper, a man who did much of the planting, helps daily with the upkeep, and is often available to answer questions about the plants. (There is an admission charge here.)

Places to Stay in Hāna Town

It is wise to make reservations well in advance of an intended overnight visit to Hāna Town. If the hotels are full, you can inquire with their reservations desks about the possibility of renting a cottage from a Hāna resident, but don't count on last-minute accommodations. There are only three regular guest facilities in the area:

The **Hotel Hana-Maui** is, of course, the most celebrated of the Hāna domiciles, and while it is also the most expensive, it should be noted that all meals are included in the hotel charge. The hotel is known worldwide for its beauty and the graciousness of its service. [On the Hāna Highway, phone (808) 321 HANA (Continental U.S.), (808) 536-7522 (direct Oahu line) or (808) 248-8211 (Maui line), or write P.O. Box 8, Hāna, HI 96713.]

Hāna Kai Resort Apartments is a lovely little enclave of oceanfront apartments, each with its own kitchen. The Hāna Kai boasts an exquisite lava rock swimming pool, fed by springs, surrounded by flower gardens and overlooking the ocean. [On the Hāna Highway, phone (808) 248-7742 or (808) 248-8426, or write P.O. Box 38, Hāna, HI 96713.]

Heavenly Hāna Inn is, truly, a heavenly

little place, surrounded by flowers and filled with antiques, with meals for guests only and a maximum capacity of 24. [On Hāna Highway before Hāna Town, phone (808) 248-8442, or write P.O. Box 146, Hāna, HI 96713.]

Places to Eat in Hāna

Tutu's at Hāna Bay is really a plate lunch stand, operating out of the Hāna Community Center on the bay. Besides saimin, mango cake, and haupia ice cream, the snack shop menu could be found at any roadside stand from Trenton, New Jersey, to Riverside, California: omelettes, hamburgers, and, of course, plate lunches. Open from 7:30 a.m. to 4:30 p.m., seven days a week.

Recently remodeled, the **Hāna Ranch Restaurant** is a tastefully appointed restaurant that sits atop a scenic knoll overlooking Hāna. Breakfast (take-out daily) is from 6:30 to 10 a.m., lunch (buffet and take-out) from 11 a.m. to 4 p.m. and dinner (Friday/ Saturday) from 6 p.m. to 9 p.m. Full bar service is available.

Featuring "California Cuisine," the **Hotel Hāna-Maui** offers an all-fresh menu. Facilities are limited when the hotel is full, so reservations are strongly suggested. The hotel is Full American Plan, so all meals are at a fixed price. [see hotel listings]

Buying the Basics

There are two stores in Hāna Town where visitors can pick up fixings for a picnic lunch, and residents, either short-term or permanent, can buy provisions for cooking their own meals:

Hāna Store, which is run by the Hāna Ranch, Inc., is just off Hāna Highway on the ranch property. The ranch store has a reasonable supply of produce and a wide assortment of well-organized foodstuff, cooking and eating implements, T-shirts, thong sandals, drugstore items, and other necessities of modern life. In addition, they offer hot and cold sandwiches, roasted chicken and all picnic necessities. They also have the only fresh meat in town. Hours are 7 a.m. to 6:30 p.m. every day.

Anything that you can't find at Hāna Store is probably sold at **Hasegawa's General Store,** the celebrated little roadside stop that contains more merchandise than we could even categorize here. Hours are 7:30 a.m. to 6 p.m. Monday through Saturday, 7:30 a.m. to 3 p.m. Sunday.

Things to Do

Of course, there is swimming, hiking, bird-watching and flower gazing, but two standout activities can be arranged through the social desk at the Hotel Hana-Maui, (808) 248-8211. The Hāna Stables, operated by the hotel, offer some of the world's most spectacular oceanside and mountain trail rides. Horses are available to fit every degree of proficiency (or lack thereof). Also call the hotel to make reservations for Hāna Bay Divers, offering dramatically colorful snorkeling and scuba-diving adventures in the protected and pristine waters of Hāna Bay.

Campsites

Camping is permitted in many parks along the Hāna Coast, and some even have cabins for "campers" who aren't really campers.
State Parks:
Kau-mahina State Park has space allotted for tent camping, with public toilets and available drinking water.

Wai-'ānapanapa State Park has both cabins and tent camping, public toilets and drinking water.

At both state parks there is a maximum stay of five nights, and a permit it required.

The permits are available only

at the Division of State Parks office in Wai-luku; they are not available in Hāna Town or at the parks themselves. [54 High Street, Wailuku, HI 96793 . . . phone (808) 244-4354]

Hale-a-ka-lā National Park (four campsites):

Hosmer Grove has an open shelter with fresh water and a chemical toilet, near the Park Headquarters. No permit is required.

Hōlua and **Pali-kū** are both inside Hale-a-ka-lā Crater, both with a cabin and tent campsite and limited drinking water.

'Ohe'o Gulch is an undeveloped campsite in the Ki-pahulu portion of the park, with open meadow camping and no drinking water.

Permits are required for camping at Hōlua, Pali'kū and 'Ohe'o and can be obtained only from the Park Headquarters, either in person on the drive up to Hale-a-ka-lā from Kula, or by mail. We suggest writing well in advance, as the cabins are very much in demand, and the privilege of using them is won by lottery, held two months in advance of the date requested. [On Haleakala Highway, phone (808) 572-9306, or write P.O. Box 369, Makawao, HI 96768]

The Kaupo Side of the Coast

It is advisable to drive from Hāna Town to 'Ohe'o Gulch (the seven pools), to Lindbergh's grave in Ki-pahulu and then back to Hāna Town and the return trip along the Ke-'anae coast, the same way you drove in. If you would like to drive back to Ka-hului through the Kau-pō side, along the Ka-naio coast, check on the condition of the road before you leave Hāna Town. The Hāna police will know.

If you do decide to brave that beautiful but rough stretch of road, there is a store in Kau-pō—the Kaupo Store—that sells essential foodstuff and a few drug-store

items — but only from 10:30 a.m. to 4:30 p.m. Monday through Friday.

A wonderful place to stop, near the end of your journey, is the **Tedeschi Vineyards and Winery** at 'Ulu-pala-kua, where you can taste their interesting pineapple and beaujolais wines and champagnes.

Going in through the Crater

If you decide to hike through Hale-a-ka-lā Crater, you may want to spend the night before in one of the two comfortable hotels on Hale-a-ka-lā Highway, just up from Kula: The **Silversword Inn** [phone (808) 878-1232] or the **Kula Lodge** [phone (808) 878-1535]

Handy Phone Numbers

Once you get to Hāna Town, addresses are actually superfluous, the place is so small that, really, you can't miss anything. But phone numbers are another matter:

Police—248-8311
Fire—911 (emergency), 248-8311
  or, if no answer, 244-7811.
Hāna Medical Center—248-8294
U.S. Coast Guard—244-5256
U.S. Post Office—248-8258
Hāna Airport—248-8208
Hāna Library—248-7714
Bank of Hawaii, Hāna
  Branch—248-8015
Hana Ranch—248-8930
Hana (Ranch) Store—248-8261
Hasegawa's General Store—248-8231

If you need to send a telegram or a telex while you are in Hāna, call Hawaiian Telephone Company's Interisland Radiogram office, toll free, at 546-3890.

And if you need to write someone in Hāna Town from anyplace else, just address it to him or her in Hāna, Hawaii, 96713, and it will get there.

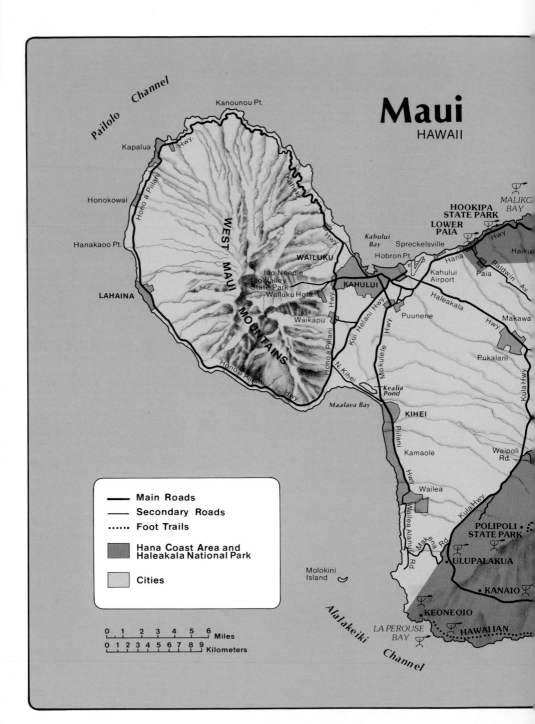

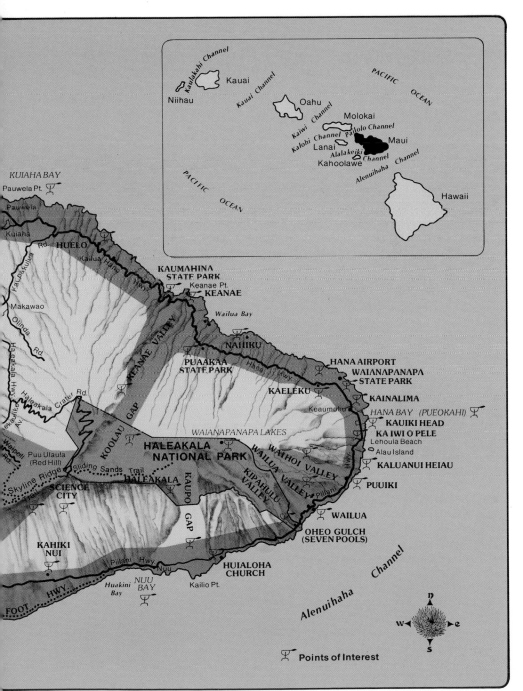

Points of Interest

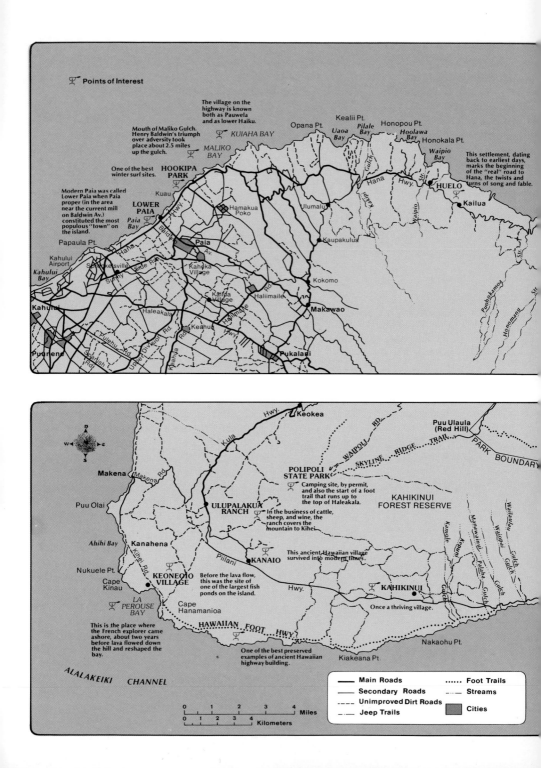

Points of Interest

The village on the highway is known both as Pauwela and as lower Haiku.

Mouth of Maliko Gulch. Henry Baldwin's triumph over adversity took place about 2.5 miles up the gulch.

KUIAHA BAY

MALIKO BAY

Opana Pt.

Kealii Pt.
Pilale Bay
Uaoa Bay
Honopou Pt.
Hoolawa Bay
Honokala Pt.

Waipio Bay

This settlement, dating back to earliest days, marks the beginning of the "real" road to Hana, the twists and turns of song and fable.

One of the best winter surf sites.

HOOKIPA PARK

Kuau

Ulumalu

Hana Hwy.

HUELO

Kailua

Modern Paia was called Lower Paia when Paia proper (in the area near the current mill on Baldwin Av.) constituted the most populous "town" on the island.

LOWER PAIA

Hamakua Poko

Paia Bay

Papaula Pt.

Baldwin Av.

Paia

Kaupakulua

Kahului Airport

Kahului Bay

Spreckelsville

Hana

Kahului

Puunene

Haleakala

Keahua

Stable Rd.

Kaheka Village

Kahua Village

Haliimaile

Kokomo

Makawao

Hulelu

Upper D. Vronot Rd.

Kahului Rd.

Haleakala Hwy.

Pukalani

Skylish Rd.

Kealii Pt.

W
N
E
S

Kula

Hwy.

Keokea

Waipoli Rd.

SKYLINE RIDGE TRAIL

Puu Ulaula (Red Hill)

PARK BOUNDARY

Makena

Makena Rd.

POLIPOLI STATE PARK

Camping site, by permit, and also the start of a foot trail that runs up to the top of Haleakala.

KAHIKINUI FOREST RESERVE

Puu Olai

ULUPALAKUA RANCH

In the business of cattle, sheep, and wine, the ranch covers the mountain to Kihei.

Ahihi Bay

Kanahena

Kihei Rd.

Pilani

KANAIO

This ancient Hawaiian village survived into modern times.

Kamole

Manawainui

Waiopai Gulch

Manawainui Gulch

Palaha Gulch

Kepuni Gulch

Nukuele Pt.

Cape Kinau

KEONEOIO VILLAGE

Before the lava flow, this was the site of one of the largest fish ponds on the island.

Hwy.

KAHIKINUI

Once a thriving village.

LA PEROUSE BAY

Cape Hanamanioa

This is the place where the French explorer came ashore, about two years before lava flowed down the hill and reshaped the bay.

HAWAIIAN FOOT HWY.

One of the best preserved examples of ancient Hawaiian highway building.

Nakaohu Pt.

Kiakeana Pt.

ALALAKEIKI CHANNEL

Main Roads	Foot Trails
Secondary Roads	Streams
Unimproved Dirt Roads	Cities
Jeep Trails	

0 1 2 3 4 Miles
0 1 2 3 4 Kilometers

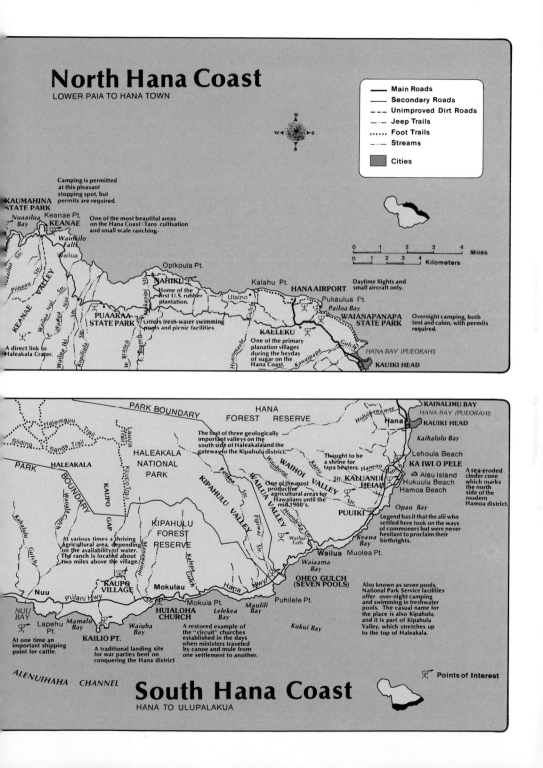

North Hana Coast
LOWER PAIA TO HANA TOWN

Legend:
- Main Roads
- Secondary Roads
- Unimproved Dirt Roads
- Jeep Trails
- Foot Trails
- Streams
- Cities

KAUMAHINA STATE PARK
Camping is permitted at this pleasant stopping spot, but permits are required.

Nuaailua Bay
KEANAE — Keanae Pt.
One of the most beautiful areas on the Hana Coast: Taro cultivation and small scale ranching.

Waiokilo Falls
Wailua

KEANAE VALLEY
A direct link to Haleakala Crater.

Piinaau Str.
Waiaha Nui Str.
Waiaha Iki Str.
Kopiliula

Opikoula Pt.

NAHIKU
Home of the first U.S. rubber plantation.

Ulaino

PUAAKAA STATE PARK
Offers fresh-water swimming pools and picnic facilities.

Kalahu Pt.   **HANA AIRPORT**   Daytime flights and small aircraft only.

Pukaulua Pt.
Pailoa Bay

WAIANAPANAPA STATE PARK
Overnight camping, both tent and cabin, with permits required.

KAELEKU
One of the primary planation villages during the heyday of sugar on the Hana Coast.

Honomaele Gulch
Kawaipapa Gulch

HANA BAY (PUEOKAHI)
KAUIKI HEAD

Scale: 0 1 2 3 4 Miles / 0 1 2 3 4 Kilometers

South Hana Coast
HANA TO ULUPALAKUA

PARK BOUNDARY
HANA FOREST RESERVE

Halemauu Trail
Lauulu Trail
Sliding Sands Trail

HALEAKALA NATIONAL PARK

PARK BOUNDARY

HALEAKALA

KAUPO

Wookoa Gulch

KAUPO GAP

Keuoa Trail

KIPAHULU FOREST RESERVE
At various times a thriving agricultural area, depending on the availability of water. The ranch is located about two miles above the village.

KIPAHULU VALLEY

WAIHOI VALLEY
The first of three geologically important valleys on the south side of Haleakala and the gateway to the Kipahulu district.

WAILUA VALLEY
One of the most productive agricultural areas for Hawaiians until the mid 1900's.

Kalepa Gulch
Manawainui Str.
Palikea Str.
Koukouai Str.
Pipiwai Str.
Honolewa Str.

Wailua Falls

KAHUANUI HEIAU
Thought to be a shrine for tapa beaters.

Hanoo Str.
Kopili Str.

PUUIKI
Legend has it that the alii who settled here took on the ways of commoners but were never hesitant to proclaim their birthrights.

Keawa Bay **Wailua** Muolea Pt.
Waiaama Bay

KAINALIMU BAY
HANA BAY (PUEOKAHI)
Hana **KAUIKI HEAD**
Kaihalulu Bay
Lehoula Beach
KA IWI O PELE
A sea-eroded cinder cone which marks the north side of the modern Hamoa district.
△ Alau Island
Hukuula Beach
Hamoa Beach
Opau Bay

OHEO GULCH (SEVEN POOLS)
Also known as seven pools, National Park Service facilities offer over-night camping and swimming in freshwater pools. The casual name for the place is also Kipahulu, and it is part of Kipahulu Valley, which stretches up to the top of Haleakala.

Puhilele Pt.

KAUPO VILLAGE
Mokulau
Pilani Hwy
Hana Hwy

NUU
Nuu Bay
Lapehu Pt.
Mamalu Bay

KAILIO PT.
A traditional landing site for war parties bent on conquering the Hana district

At one time an important shipping point for cattle.

Waiuha Bay

HUIALOHA CHURCH
A restored example of the "circuit" churches established in the days when ministers traveled by canoe and mule from one settlement to another.

Mokuia Pt.
Lelekea Bay
Maulili Bay
Kukui Bay

ALENUIHAHA CHANNEL

🍖 **Points of Interest**

Puu
Nianiau
6849

Hosmer Grove
Camp Grounds

Ranger
Station

Haleakala Hwy.

Rain
Shed

Trail
Parking

Crater
Overlook

Cave

Holua
Cabin

Kalahaku
Overlook

Halemauu

KOOLAU GAP

Begins at the top of the
Keanae Valley and runs
all the way to the sea
at Keanae Peninsula.

Waikau
Cabin

Silversword
Loop

Puu
Kumu

Hanakauli
8907

Mauna Hina

Puu Mamane

Halemauu

Trail

Halalii

Puu O Maui

Ka Moa
O Pele

Puu
Naue

Puu Ulaula
(Red Hill)

Observatory

Kamaoli

HALEAKALA CRATER

Puu Maile

A collection of
observatories and
communications
facilities.

SCIENCE
CITY

Magnetic Peak
10,008

Kolekole
10,012

Sliding   Sands   Trail

Haupaakea Peak
9159

PARK   BOUNDARY

HALEAKAL
8201

SKYLINE RIDGE TRAIL

Closed to vehicles because
dust would be injurious to
scientific studies conducted
at observatories.

This mount used by the
demi-god Maui when
he snared the sun.

KAHIKINUI FOREST RESERVE

N
W   E
S

0   1/2   1   2   3   4
Miles

0   1/2 1   2   3   4
Kilometers

545 Elevation in Feet

Haleakala National Park

Unusual fresh-water lakes located at the about 7,000-foot level of the mountain and inaccessible except by air.

HANA
FOREST RESERVE

WAIANAPANAPA LAKES

KALAPAWILI RIDGE

Laie Cave

Oili Puu

Palike Cabin

Kuiki
7553

KIPAHULU

VALLEY

KAUPO
GAP

A trail runs down from the crater through the gap into Kaupo Village. It's a strenuous hike.

KIPAHULU
FOREST RESERVE

PARK

BOUNDARY

Waimoku
Falls

Gulch

Alenuihaha Channel

	Main Roads
	Secondary Roads
·····	Foot Trails
—·—	Streams
⚑	Points of Interest

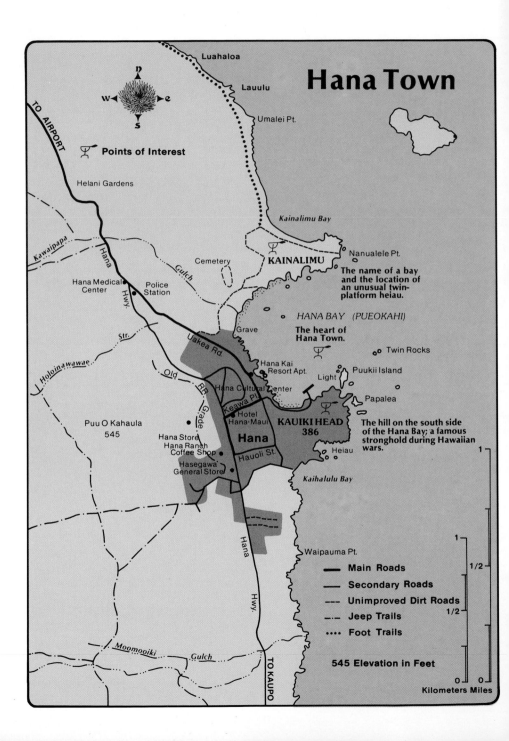

Hana Town

Luahaloa

Lauulu

Umalei Pt.

Kainalimu Bay

Nanualele Pt.

KAINALIMU

The name of a bay and the location of an unusual twin-platform heiau.

HANA BAY (PUEOKAHI)

The heart of Hana Town.

Twin Rocks

Puukii Island

Papalea

KAUIKI HEAD 386

The hill on the south side of the Hana Bay; a famous stronghold during Hawaiian wars.

Heiau

Kaihalulu Bay

Waipauma Pt.

Grave

Hana Kai Resort Apt.

Light

Hana Cultural Center

Keawa Pt.

Hotel Hana-Maui

Hana

Hauoli St.

Hana Store
Hana Ranch Coffee Shop
Hasegawa General Store

Puu O Kahaula
545

Old RR Grade

Uakea Rd.

Grave

Hana Medical Center

Police Station

Cemetery

Gulch

Helani Gardens

TO AIRPORT

Kawaipapa

Hana Hwy.

Holoinawawae

Str.

Hana Hwy.

TO KAUPO

Moomooiki

Gulch

🔱 **Points of Interest**

Main Roads

Secondary Roads

Unimproved Dirt Roads

Jeep Trails

Foot Trails

545 Elevation in Feet

Kilometers Miles

1

1/2

1

1/2

0   0

N
W — E
S

SELECTED HANA BIBLIOGRAPHY

Beckwith, Martha
Hawaiian Mythology. Honolulu: The
University Press of Hawaii, 1982.
*The Kumulipo, a Hawaiian Creation
Chant.* Chicago: University of Chicago
Press, 1951.

Chinen, Jon
The Great Mahele. Honolulu: The
University Press of Hawaii, 1958.

Chisholm, Craig
Hawaiian Hiking Trails. The
Touchstone Press, Beaverton,
Oregon, 1977.

Clark, John R. K.
The Beaches of Maui County.
Honolulu: The University Press
of Hawaii, 1980.

Cordy, Ross
*Piilanihale Heiau Project, Phase I Site
Report.* Honolulu: Bernice P. Bishop
Museum, Department of Anthropology,
Report 70-9, 1970.

**Department of Geography,
University of Hawaii**
Atlas of Hawaii. Honolulu: The
University Press of Hawaii, 1973.

Forster, John
*Acculturation of Hawaiians on the
Island of Maui, Hawaii.* Los Angeles:
University of California at Los Angeles
Press, 1959.

Fornander, Abraham
Hawaiian Antiquities and Folk-lore.
Honolulu: Bernice P. Bishop Museum
Memoirs. Vols. 4, 5, 1917, 1918.

Gassner, Julius S. (translator)
Voyages and Adventures of La Perouse.
Honolulu: The University Press
of Hawaii, 1969.

Handy, E. S. Craighill
*The Hawaiian Planter, His Plants,
Methods and Areas of Cultivation.*
Honolulu: Bernice P. Bishop Museum
Bulletin 161, 1940.

Ii, John Papa
Fragments of Hawaiian History.
Honolulu: Bernice P. Bishop Museum
Press, 1959.

Kamakau, Samuel Manaiakalani,
Ruling Chiefs of Hawaii. Honolulu:
Kamehameha Schools Press, 1961.

Kyselka, Will
with Ray Lanterman, *Maui, How It
Came to Be.* Honolulu: The University
Press of Hawaii, 1980.

**LaPerouse, Jean Francois de Galaup,
Comte de**
*A Voyage Round the World, Performed
in the Years 1785, 1786, 1787, and
1788 By the Boussoule and Astrolabe.*
New York: Da Capo Press, 1968.

Luomala, Katharine
*Maui-of-a-Thousand-Tricks; His
Oceanic and European Biographers.*
Honolulu: Bernice P. Bishop Museum
Bulletin 203, 1949.

Malo, David
Hawaiian Antiquities. Honolulu:
Bernice P. Bishop Museum Special
Publications 2. (First edition translated
by Nathaniel Emerson in 1898.), 1951.

Pukui, Mary Kawena
with Samuel H. Elbert and Esther T.
Mookini, *Place Names of Hawaii.*
Honolulu: The University Press
of Hawaii, 1981.

Thrum, Thomas G.
The Hawaiian Almanac and Annual,
Honolulu: Thomas G. Thrum, 1884,
1896, 1901, 1902.

Walker, Winslow M.
Maui Survey (1930) (typed copy).
Honolulu: Bernice P. Bishop Museum
Anthropology Department, N.D.

Wenkam, Robert
Maui No Ka Oi. Chicago: Rand
McNally, 1980.

INDEX/GLOSSARY

CREDITS